The Murder of Prime Minister Spencer Perceval

A Portrait of the Assassin

The Murder of Prime Minister Spencer Perceval

A Portrait of the Assassin

Martin Connolly

PEN & SWORD HISTORY

AN IMPRINT OF PEN & SWORD BOOKS LTD.
YORKSHIRE – PHILADELPHIA

First published in Great Britain in 2018 by
PEN AND SWORD HISTORY
an imprint of
Pen & Sword Books Ltd
Yorkshire - Philadelphia

Hardback ISBN: 978 1 52673 124 1
Paperback ISBN: 978 1 52675 147 8

Printed and bound in England
By TJ International Ltd.

Pen & Sword Books Ltd incorporates the Imprints of Pen & Sword Books
Archaeology, Atlas, Aviation, Battleground, Discovery, Family History,
History, Maritime, Military, Naval, Politics, Railways, Select, Transport,
True Crime, Fiction, Frontline Books, Leo Cooper, Praetorian Press,
Seaforth Publishing, Wharncliffe and White Owl.

For a complete list of Pen & Sword titles please contact

PEN & SWORD BOOKS LIMITED
47 Church Street, Barnsley, South Yorkshire, S70 2AS, England
E-mail: enquiries@pen-and-sword.co.uk
Website: www.pen-and-sword.co.uk
or
PEN AND SWORD BOOKS
1950 Lawrence Rd, Havertown, PA 19083, USA
E-mail: Uspen-and-sword@casematepublishers.com

'The immense drains upon the country at large (and Mr. Perceval's budget for this year was to have added Two Millions to the taxes) for the support of the war in Spain, amounting to Twenty Millions a year, with a diminished prospect of success; while the Orders in Council shut us out of almost every port in Europe and America, have alienated the hearts of nine tenths of the people from public measures, if not from public men:– hence, brooding in secret, over calamities apparently irremediable, the spirits of revenge, rapine, and assassination, have stalked abroad in open daylight; and, instead of being dreaded and detested as heretofore, seem to be viewed by the people with levity and indifference, if not with secret satisfaction: as if the shocking devastations they have produced, were only a just retaliation upon those, whom it is supposed are daily heaping distress upon public bodies equally with private individuals.'

Charles Verulam Williams Esq. 1812

Contents

Acknowledgements

I am always amazed at how helpful so many people are to authors. I would like to acknowledge the assistance of the staff at the British Library and the National Archives. As ever, I found them helpful and considerate and always willing to help and advise. I am also grateful to the many organisations that allowed the use of images, which help to illustrate the text.

Note:

All historical sums of money (shown in brackets throughout) were calculated for 2017 through the Bank of England's calculator:
www.bankofengland.co.uk/education/Pages/resources/inflationtools/calculator/default.aspx

Preface

An assassination of a politician in England has only occurred once. It was at a time when the world order was going through another period of rapid change. From the seeds of the industrial revolution in 1712, when Thomas Newcomen made steam engines to pump water from mines, progress would see further developments of the application of steam. With the advance of mechanisation came trouble as well as progress. The country would move from an agricultural economy to one where mechanisation would draw people from the rural centres into the towns and cities. There would be the dawning of concerns to develop education, health and improve the condition of the poor.

After a trough in religious belief, in the mid-eighteenth century England would see a revival of religious fervour, through George Whitefield, that touched even the highest offices of state. He was an English Anglican cleric who with John and Charles Wesley founded Methodism and the evangelical movement. Born in Gloucester, he matriculated at Pembroke College at the University of Oxford in 1732.

There was also the continued debate, argument and violence of Catholic emancipation. America, France, Ireland were all embroiled with Great Britain as the ideas of freedom of men and countries moved from philosophical debate to the force of arms. This would bring about great social changes in many areas, particularly the lot of slaves and workers.

England had always bred men and women who were ambitious in business and wealth accumulation. They would travel the globe to spread the Empire and create vast wealth for themselves which would allow the establishment of palatial estates back home. The nineteenth century saw many embark on such adventures and it was this that drew one particular man to Russia, where he hoped to fulfil his own dreams and share in this wealth. His failure to do so would result in tragedy as he became desperate in his shattered illusions. He would experience great hardships, often self-imposed, and would lose himself in a fatal quest to reverse his fortune.

The religiously inspired Prime Minister of England, as the eighteenth century gave way to the nineteenth, focused on crusades to reform society. He would insist on his own way believing it was divinely inspired. He would refuse to assist our failed fortune seeker. The two men would wind their way on very different roads in life, one a happily married and contented man with many children and given many privileges, rising to the high offices of state and power. The other a troubled man who, from a tragic childhood, struggled through life with a family he rarely saw. For this man in particular, there were no privileges. He staggered from one failure

'No Popery' rioters in Palace Yard, Parliament 1780.

to another. He would seek to rise to great heights but ended as a man familiar with prisons as an inmate, ultimately to die at the end of a noose.

A century after Newcomen's steam breakthrough, our unfortunate and failed businessman wanted his own breakthrough to wealth. His path and that of the privileged man of state converged in the Lobby of the Houses of Parliament on 11 May 1812. The events of their meeting that day would establish a chapter in British history that never will be forgotten. The death of one and the trial of the other has been the concern of a few works that focus on the assassination that happened that day. What of the background of the then relatively unknown man who brought death to Parliament? The book does not set out to excuse or defend but to describe and explain. With fresh material from the archives it gives a detailed portrait of an assassin.

Chapter 1

A Background of War and Violence

America was the setting for a proxy war between England and France. The indigenous people were forced into a 'civil war' having to decide on whose side they would fight. The eventual slicing up of territory between the French and English never settled the underlying problems of the country. By 1783, America was in revolutionary fever; the British had now become a distant authority imposing their own ideas of 'democracy' from George III's parliament. This effectively excluded the local people from any say in their taxation or governance and bloody conflict saw England lose its American colonies. Meanwhile, France itself lurched on, with its own people growing in dissatisfaction with 'democracy'. On 21 January 1793, the guillotine falling on the neck of Louis XVI sent a shockwave throughout Europe. In England, the rights of man being promoted elsewhere threatened the very heart of a monarchy that itself had known regicide. By 1799, the madness of the French revolution was abating as Napoleon Bonaparte took command and turned his sights on war with England. Wellington was sent to Portugal to attack France, but was unable to break the French battle lines, finding himself bogged down. Rumours of French spies ran like wildfire throughout England and with the expense of Wellington's army was creating an unprecedented drain on the British Exchequer, the government's opponents were in full cry to bring them home.

America, not long distant from her independence, had become frustrated at the lack of diplomatic progress on what was perceived as British aggression on the high seas. The British government's Orders in Council in 1807 were invoked to take action against France and her allies on the high seas. The British enforced a policy of boarding any ship, whether enemy or neutral, and removing anyone suspected of being a British citizen; they then would be press-ganged into the Navy. Any goods considered contraband would also be seized. British ships created blockades on French ports. Any vessel to or from them would be stopped and goods seized; naturally, France retaliated against British bound ships and trade ground to a halt with devastating effects in Britain and America. The embargo paralysed the docks in Liverpool, London and New York. The Orders allowed the government of the day to adjust policy without the need for full parliamentary approval. The merchant classes in England and America were seeing their capital

LOUIS XVI. avoit mis le Bonnet rouge, il avoit crié vive la nation, il avoit bu a la santé des sans-culotte, il avoit affecté le plus grand calme, il avoit dit hautement qu'il ne craindroit jamais, que jamais il n'auroit à craindre au milieu du peuple ; enfin il avoit semblé prendre une part personnelle à l'insurrection du 20 juin. Eh bien! ce même Louis XVI. a bravement attendu que ses concitoyens fussent rentrés dans leurs foyers pour leur faire une guerre occulte et exercer sa vengeance.

A satirical sketch of a drunken Louis XVI referring to the 'Tennis Court Oath' of his opposition. The French comment speaks of the National Committee's defiance of him '"The same Louis XVI who bravely waits until his fellow citizens' return to their hearths to plan a secret war and exact his revenge."

tied up in warehouses bulging with unshipped cargoes and their profits wiped out. Their anger was directed at the British government and more specifically Spencer Perceval for using the Order in Council mechanism. Perceval had also brought in heavy taxation to finance his war with France. That same government was also at war with the slave traders who saw their lucrative trade destroyed by the aggressive seizing of ships and slaves being released. Even ships operating from foreign ports were not excluded from the reach of the English battle against the trade. Workers were thrown out of employment into poverty; in December 1811 the king issued a proclamation against workers in

NAPOLEON BUONAPARTE.   FROM AN AUTHENTIC PORTRAIT.

Napoleon Bonaparte.

the stocking trade at Nottingham. They were using 'force and violence' in their opposition to changes in wages and working practices. The proclamation offered £50

Boarding and Taking the American Ship Chesapeake, by the Officers & Crew of H.M. Ship Shannon, Commanded by Capt. Broke, June 1813. Painted by Charles Heath. Anne S. K. Brown Military Collection, Brown University Library, Providence, Rhode Island.

SPENCER PERCEVAL. FROM AN AUTHENTIC PORTRAIT.

An early portrait of Spencer Perceval.

(£3,700) for information leading to the arrest of any 'agitators'. Notices and weavers' petitions appeared, calling on change from the Government. Britain was an angry country.

The Orders in Council, exorbitant taxes and the Poor Laws were beginning to put many workers into destitution. Families with hunger in their belly and fathers feeling impotent to help drove them into a violent rage; the people were literally up in arms confronting the militia and other agents of the law. Rioting, destruction of property and the murder of business owners were common. By 1812, the British government was the object of fury from all these interested parties, who came from every sector of society, at home and abroad. The echoes of the French revolution created the greatest of concern in high places and the declaration of war by America and the attacks on Canadian soil threw the merchant class into deeper anger. George III was a devoted husband and father who had reigned over a country that had experienced much political instability and he watched the struggle for American independence and the loss of the colonies with great sadness. The French, Spanish and Dutch had joined in alliance with America and England's government had neither allies abroad nor many friends at home; the country was heading for a constitutional crisis. George III had struggled with illness and his mental state deteriorated to the point that in 1798 steps were taken to appoint his unpopular son as regent. This process was bogged down by political arguments and by the time it was resolved, George had recovered sufficiently to regain his authority. The French revolution was a shocking event for him and the ongoing political instability meant he could never rest easy. By 1810, he had again descended into madness and his over-indulged son, George, had become Prince Regent. He was unpopular; trapped in an unhappy marriage and with many mistresses, he accrued debts and was not effective as an authority. Parliament began to assert its own power and struggled with the great social issues of the day but the Prince Regent was the man on whom the country's anger focused, along with his appointed First Minister and Lord of the Treasury, Spencer Perceval.

17

A NOTICE. *20.th April 1812*

To WEAVERS, SPINNERS, MECHANICS, *and Others,* the Inhabitants of the Town and Neighbourhood of CHORLEY.

A PETITION to the Honorable the House of Commons of the the United Kingdom of Great Britain and Ireland, (of which the following is a Copy), is offered for the Signature of those to whose Cases it may apply: and you he Inhabitants aforesaid are hereby informed, that this Petition well be open for the Signature of such of you as may approve of its Contents, at the House of *James Marsgnall* N.º *81 Bottom* street in Chorley, between the Hours of six and nine o'Clock in the Evening of every Day, until the *first* Day of *May* next.

It offers to those of you who particularly feel the Pressure of the present calamitous Times, a legal, constitutional, and proper Mode of making your Situations known to that Source, whence you have a Right to expect Relief.

To the Honourable the Commons of the United Kingdom of Great Britain and Ireland in Parliament assembled.

THE Humble PETITION of the undersigned Weavers, and other Working Manufacturers, of the Town of CHORLEY and the Neighbourhood thereof, SHEWETH, That your Petitioners have been for a long time labouring under a State of the utmost Distress; as your Honourable House will easily conceive, on being informed, that whereas the Price of the Necessaries of Life has been nearly doubled since the Commencement of Hostilities with France in 1793, the Wages of your Petitioners are reduced two thirds.

THAT in these afflicting Circumstances the Feelings of your Petitioners are greatly aggravated by their Knowledge, that whilst their utmost Exertions in Labour cannot save them from starving, vast Sums of the Public Money are bestowed upon Individuals, as the Salaries of Sinecure Places:—that is to say, of Places, the Holders of which receive Wages without performing any Work for the same.

THAT in Proof of their Assertion, that vast Sums of the Public Money are thus bestowed, selecting a few Instances out of a great Variety of the same Nature, they beg leave to remind your Honorable House, that the Right Honorable GEORGE ROSE holds the Sinecure Office of Clerk of the Parliament, with a Salary of £8,278 per Annum;—that the Right Honorable CHARLES GEORGE Lord ARDEN holds the Sinecure Offices of Register of the High Court of Admiralty, and of Register of the High Court of Appeal for Prizes, for which he receives, clear of Deductions, £12,534 per Annum;—and that the Earl CAMDEN, and the Marquis of *Buckingham*, hold the Sinecure Offices of Tellers of the Exchequer, for which Offices they receive,—the latter £23,093, the former, £23,117 per Annum.

THAT your Petitioners have from Time to Time been informed of large Sums of Money being paid out of the Public Purse to distressed Foreigners; on which Head, passing by the Sums paid as Subsidies to the Portuguese and Sicilian Courts,—to the Duke and Duchess of BRUNSWICK, and divers other German Refugees, they beg Leave to call to the Recollection of your Honorable House the Sums paid to the exiled Catholic Clergy and Laity of France, which amounted in the Year

1794 to	£ 99,548 7 6		1798 to	£161,333 7 0
1795 to	£135,890 0 0		1799 to	£187,886 10 11
1796 to	£199,890 0 0		1800 to	£195,713 5 1
1797 to	£177,480 9 7		1801 to	£180,772 0 0

THAT though your Petitioners presume to be of Opinion that in the Season of their Distress they have as strong a Claim upon the Public Purse of the Nation as any Foreigners whatsoever; and though they are apprised that the Precedent of the special Distribution in the Year 1801, of £24,226, to the Parishes where the Weaving of Silk is carried on in LONDON, would justify them in applying to your Honorable House for direct pecuniary Relief, they deem it more becoming them as Englishmen to declare to your Honorable House, that they would far prefer to the Receipt of any extraordinary Assistance, a Dependence upon their own unimpeded Industry; and that they therefore do respectfully, but earnestly, call upon the Members of your Honorable House well to consider the Premises,—and by the Powers by the Constitution vested in your Honorable House, to check and restrain the extravagant Expenditure of the Public Money; which, by occasioning the Imposition of enormous Taxes, increases the Price of the Necessaries of Life,—and to compel His Majesty's Ministers to adopt a Line of Policy, which, by conciliating Neutral Nations, may effect the Revival of Trade; which alone, by renewing the Strength of the Nation, can, under the Divine Providence, finally secure to us the Blessing of an Honorable and Lasting Peace.

[Walker, Printer, Preston.]

The Weavers' Notice and Petition.

George III.

Perceval was born on 1 November 1762. He had the privilege of background that took him through public school and into Trinity College, Cambridge. The MA he achieved there took him to a career at the Bar, eventually obtaining silk. After this, he was given preferment to the lofty position of Master of the Rolls in 1801 and then onto Attorney-General, eventually becoming Chief Justice. Perceval had ambition in politics and the death of his uncle, the 8th Earl of Northampton, brought his ambitions to fulfilment in 1796 when Perceval's cousin, the MP for Northampton, succeeded his father and entered the House of Lords. The Northampton seat went to Perceval unopposed; however, within a matter of weeks he was called to defend his seat in a general election. The contest was close and after a disputed count Perceval was elected. Perceval never had to face another election, continually being returned unopposed thereafter. His concerns were mainly those of finance and the influence of Catholics, which he opposed. Although encouraging toleration in religion, he was steadfastly active in opposition to the Irish Catholic aims in Ireland.

A devoted husband and father, he had married Jane Wilson in 1790. Her father Sir Thomas Spencer Wilson opposed the marriage and the couple eloped to be married. Perceval was an evangelical Christian from the Clapham sect, a fellowship of Church of England social reformers who based themselves in Clapham, London from around the 1780s. Among them were John Newton, a former Royal Navy captain and involved in the shipping of slaves. He had a religious experience that brought

The Prince Regent.

The Clapham Sect.

his conversion and abandoning of the slave trade and he became a Minister in the Church of England joining anti-slavery campaigners. He was a major influence on Perceval. William Wilberforce, a politician who was also passionate in opposing the slave trade and demanding its total ban across the world, was also at the heart of the group. This group were a very powerful band of Christian evangelicals who were bound together by common moral and spiritual values. They had a religious mission that spurred them to social activism and Perceval was convinced that God had placed him where he was. This informed all his decisions and reinforced his

unbending refusal to stop his attacks on shipping, the slave trade and to repeal other legislation he had placed on the statute books. There was much unhappiness about the influence this group were having on Perceval's decisions. It was when the Duke of Portland was in office that Perceval was asked to become Chancellor of the Exchequer, Leader of the House of Commons and Duchy of Lancaster; it was through this office that he promoted many of the causes of the sect to which he belonged. In 1809, he was appointed Prime Minister by George III, though he was not the first choice and the role was seen as a poisoned chalice because of the huge problems facing the nation. No one could be found

John Newton by Joseph Collyer the Younger, after John Russell.

Sir Francis Burdett MP

to take on the role of Chancellor and so Perceval continued the role without the salary that came with it. This was in line with his deep religious convictions against greed and seeking after mammon. On his death, he left only £100 (£6,500) in his bank account, a very modest sum for a man in his position. As his term in office continued, so did the opposition to his policies.

It was therefore in these circumstances that he had three countries angry with his role on the international stage; America, France and Ireland. Add to this the internal problems of the country and we see conditions in which revolution was a possibility. Anonymous pamphlets and posters began to appear, openly calling for the death of both the Prince Regent and Prime Minister. Indeed, the graphic nature of the threats was seen in those who would 'roast the Regent's heart on the ribs of Perceval'. In 1810, a riot over the arrest of Sir Francis Burdett in London was quelled and several people were killed by the military. Burdett was a radical demanding reform of the whole political system. It was symptomatic of the unhappiness and unrest in the country; violence was now a normal response to grievances. The lot of the common man at one end of the scale was pitiful whilst at the other end the wealthy merchants seethed at government interference on their trade that affected profits; nervousness was over the whole population and Parliament sought a way to prevent a spark igniting revolution.

So it was that on 11 May 1812, a debate began in the Houses of Parliament to address the most pressing of these problems; the repeal of the Orders that were blocking trade. Spencer Perceval seemed unconcerned as he made his leisurely way to the Commons, late for the start of the debate. He had a great confidence in his own righteous position as he stepped into the Lobby to take the fight to his opponents. A tall 'raw-boned man with a long thin visage and aquiline nose around forty-two years of age', with deep blue eyes, and dark curly hair, waited within the Lobby. He stepped forward to meet Perceval, he was dressed 'like a decent mechanic', with a large brown overcoat that covered a fashionable gentleman's morning attire. He drew a pistol from within his coat and fired a ball of lead from a flintlock pistol into Perceval's heart. The Prime Minister cried, 'Murder …

Riot of Burdett supporters.

Contemporary sketch of the assassination of Spencer Perceval.

Oh, God!' and in minutes he was dead. The first assassination of a British Prime Minister would solve the problems of many factions and powerful merchants. Who was the man who pulled the trigger in this dreadful act? What had brought him to this appointment with history? Did he act alone or was he an agent of others?

Chapter 2

Born Into Madness

William Scarbrow was a reasonably well-off country gentleman living in St Neots in Huntingdonshire. With his wife, Mary, he had made a good living from his business and owned a few properties in the town. Well respected and a regular member of St Mary's church, he lived, as he would record, 'in the fear of God'. Being blessed with children, he would see three daughters and a son come into this world; Stephen, Frances, Mary and Elizabeth. As a good Christian, he had imparted his faith to his wife and children and she would bring them up in the same fear of God he had embraced.

We do not know what it was that made his daughter Elizabeth unsettled in her country existence. Perhaps her contemporary Jane Austen points to a reason, 'It is a truth universally acknowledged, that a single man in possession of a good fortune must be in want of a wife'? Such a single man did not appear to be available for Elizabeth in the provincial St Neots and therefore, when she reached the age of majority and her inheritance of the sum of £50 (£10,000) from her father was realised, she made her way to the great city of London. There, with the help of her family contacts William Wye and his family, she established herself.

However it happened, Elizabeth found herself in the charming company of an artist, a miniature portrait painter to be more exact. How he, as a struggling painter, reacted to a girl with a substantial bank balance can only be speculated. However, we can imagine the excitement of a young girl of twenty-two, being immersed in this new culture. Swept off her feet by the charms of John Bellingham, her artist, on 8 May 1767 they entered into a marriage bond of 'two hundred pounds of good and lawful money of Great Britain' promising to marry. Four days later, that promise was fulfilled in the church of St Martin's in the Fields. Eliza Wye and Rich Lacey acted as their witnesses. On 19 April 1768, a daughter, Mary, was born and on 19 November 1772, her brother John joined the family.

Initially, John Bellingham senior seemed to enjoy a modicum of success with his miniatures, even having them in a prominent exhibition. The Society of British Artists lists two of his works in their records in 1767 and 1768. We can wonder if the 'miniature of a lady' displayed, was the lovely Elizabeth, his new love. This success was short lived and it appears that pressure was great on him as he was beginning to show signs of mental strain. In 1773, the family returned to St Neots for a quieter

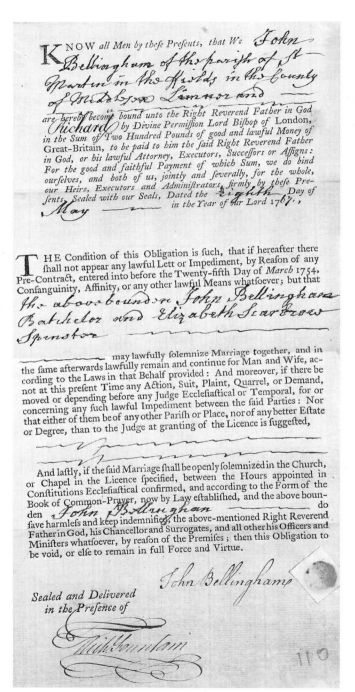

KNOW all Men by these Presents, that We *John Bellingham of the parish of St Martin in the fields in the County of Middlesex Gunner and* are hereby become bound unto the Right Reverend Father in God *Richard* by Divine Permission Lord Bishop of London, in the Sum of Two Hundred Pounds of good and lawful Money of Great-Britain, to be paid to him the said Right Reverend Father in God, or his lawful Attorney, Executors, Successors or Assigns: For the good and faithful Payment of which Sum, we do bind ourselves, and both of us, jointly and severally, for the whole, our Heirs, Executors and Administrators, firmly by these Presents, Sealed with our Seals, Dated the *eighth* Day of *May* in the Year of our Lord 176*7*.

THE Condition of this Obligation is such, that if hereafter there shall not appear any lawful Lett or Impediment, by Reason of any Pre-Contract, entered into before the Twenty-fifth Day of *March* 1754, Consanguinity, Affinity, or any other lawful Means whatsoever; but that *the above bounden John Bellingham Batchelor and Elizabeth Scarbrow Spinster* may lawfully solemnize Marriage together, and in the same afterwards lawfully remain and continue for Man and Wife, according to the Laws in that Behalf provided: And moreover, if there be not at this present Time any Action, Suit, Plaint, Quarrel, or Demand, moved or depending before any Judge Ecclesiastical or Temporal, for or concerning any such lawful Impediment between the said Parties: Nor that either of them be of any other Parish or Place, nor of any better Estate or Degree, than to the Judge at granting of the Licence is suggested,

And lastly, if the said Marriage shall be openly solemnized in the Church, or Chapel in the Licence specified, between the Hours appointed in Constitutions Ecclesiastical confirmed, and according to the Form of the Book of Common-Prayer, now by Law established, and the above bounden *John Bellingham* do save harmless and keep indemnified, the above-mentioned Right Reverend Father in God, his Chancellor and Surrogates, and all other his Officers and Ministers whatsoever, by reason of the Premises; then this Obligation to be void, or else to remain in full Force and Virtue.

John Bellingham

Sealed and Delivered
in the Presence of

The marriage bond of Bellingham's parents showing the agreement to marry.

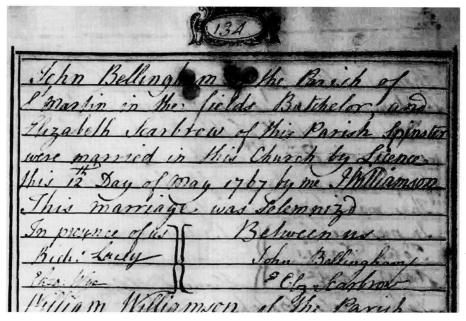

The Parish Record of Bellingham's father's marriage to Elizabeth.

life. The young John Bellingham junior was always brought up in the same tradition as his mother. In St Neots, as he grew, he enjoyed the freshness of the countryside and found great companionship with his cousin, Ann Scarbrow His mother would continue to look to her religion and young John would be read the Bible and join in family prayers. Later in life he would be found often quoting Biblical verses in his arguments and justifications. His education was not neglected and he developed well in the areas of mathematics and English. Later he would claim, for sympathy, to be poorly educated but the evidence does not support that claim.

We can begin to see in this background a young boy of good intelligence learning about what was right and wrong. He would be brought up in the understanding of justice and the penalties of sinning against righteousness. His Bible would have informed him of the principles of 'an eye for an eye' and of the punishment for

Bellingham's baptismal entry.

1770.   23 A View of Brougham Castle in Cumberland.

24 A View of Warwick-hall, under an arch of the bridge, in Cumberland.

1771.   8 A View of Lord's Island and Derwentwater.

9 A View from the Park of Lord's Island and Derwentwater.

10 A View of Bywell Bay in Northumberland.

11 A View of the ruin of Penrith Castle in Cumberland.

1772.   9 A View of the great cascade at Corby Castle in Cumberland.

10 A sunset.

11 A moonlight.

12   do.

13 A storm; a drawing.

239 Head of our Saviour; in crayons.

240 A landscape, sun rising.

241 A sunset.

1773.   17 A View of Derwentwater in Cumberland.

18 A View of a small lake in Sussex.

19 A View towards Cumberland Fort, Hampshire.

BELLEW, Captain ... ... Painter.
SOCIETY OF ARTISTS.
(An Honorary Exhibitor.)

1764.   218 A View of the Havanna; India Ink.

219 Five miniatures.

1767.   293 Two portraits from life; in miniature.

294 Landscape; compositions

BELLINGHAM...Miniature Painter.
SOCIETY OF ARTISTS.
At Mr. Ingall's,
opposite Round Court, Strand.

1766.   10 A miniature of a lady.

1767.   8 Portrait of a gentleman; in miniature.

BELLOTTI ... ... Painter.
SOCIETY OF ARTISTS.
At Mr. Grant's,
in Cross Street,
Carnaby Market.

1765.   6 A piece of ruins.

BEMBRIDGE ... ... Painter.
In Italy.
FREE SOCIETY.

1769.   258 Pascal Paoli, the general of the Corsicans; a whole length.

BEMFLEET, G. ... ... Painter.
SOCIETY OF ARTISTS.
At Mr. Mountstevens,
Great Wild Street,
Long Acre.

1772.   33 Narcissus.

BENAZECH, Charles ... ... Painter.
SOCIETY OF ARTISTS.

1761.   176 A View.

1762.   165 A Landscape from Pillement.

166 Its companion.

BENCRAFT ... ... Painter.
FREE SOCIETY.

1783.   9 A scene in the Fair Penitent.

BENEFIALI, Cavaliere Marco.
Painter.
FREE SOCIETY.
Chevalier Benofiali.

1780.   217 Angelica and Medora.

BENEFIALI, Chevalier (a Disciple of) ... ... Painter.
FREE SOCIETY.

1779.   192 A Turkish lady on a sopha attended by a black eunuch.

193 A Turkish lady on a sopha playing on a guitar.

194 A Turk, contractor for the Army.

195 A Turk borrowing money on his bond from a Jew usurer.

196 An Italian physician feeling his patient's pulse.

197 Italian courtship, or the cisibec at the toilette of his lady.

198 An Italian concert.

199 A rural scene in Italy.

BENNETT ... ... Painter.
FREE SOCIETY.
100, Oxford Street.

1783.   192 A Tyger.

BENWELL, Miss Mary (afterwards Mrs. Code)...Miniature Painter, etc.
SOCIETY OF ARTISTS.

1762.   4 Four heads; in crayons.

5 Four miniatures.

1763.   10 A lady; in oil, half length.

11 Portrait of a lady; in crayons.

12   do.   do.   do.

13 A child with flowers.

14 Three miniatures.

John Bellingham Senior's exhibition entry.

Excerpt from the records of the London Bethlehem Hospital, showing the entry for Bellingham's father.

those who acted unjustly. As he joined Ann in the green meadows around his home and watched the comings and goings of the local markets, even at a young age his agile mind would begin to form ideas of his future.

However, there was also his father, whose mental state was deteriorating. Young John would watch the concerned face of his mother, growing more anxious as her husband worsened. He would also see the local authority refuse to take responsibility for an outsider from London. The result of this was the six-year-old John with his sister Mary, would have to return to London. They moved to Great Titchfield Street, from where young John would continue his education. All did not go well with his father's health. Later it would be reported that John senior was placed into St Luke's Hospital for Lunatics This was a place where the more affluent would

A scene from William Hogarth's The Rake's Progress, depicting inmates at Bethlehem Royal Hospital. Wellcome Library, London

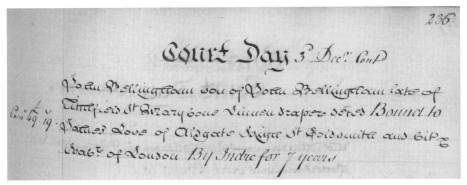

Entry in the Apprentice Rolls for John Bellingham.

find rest for their troubled souls. A complete search of the records of St Luke's Hospital has no record of John Bellingham senior's admission but in any case, the family finances were now low, with Elizabeth's money nearly exhausted. Young John had to watch his father delivered to the chaos that was London Bethlehem Hospital, later nicknamed 'Bedlam'. Their records show his admission on 24 July 1779 and his discharge on 12 February 1780 as 'sick and weak'. By June of that year he would be dead and buried from his home in Great Titchfield Street. Young John was only 8 years of age. With the loss of his father, he would now be found in the company of his mother and sister for the next four years. There can be no doubt that he would be smothered in love by his doting mother and, later evidence would suggest, spoiled and wont to have his own demanding way.

Elizabeth was not entirely left alone in the world. She had relations who still took an interest in her and her two fatherless children. One such was William Daw, her sister Mary's husband. They had no children and looked fondly on young John and Mary. At the age of 12, on 31 Dec 1783, William took John along to a friend and business colleague, James Love who ran a 'Goldsmith and Hardware-man and Draper's shop' on Aldgate High Street, London. The Apprentice Record shows that William paid the principal sum of £49 19s (£6,800) to bind John to Mr Love for 'the term of 7 years'. This sponsorship was a generous gesture and afforded the John with an opportunity to develop good business skills in a very respectable trade.

However, we now begin to see the flaws in his character. He spurned the chance he had been given and abandoned his apprenticeship three years later. What happened next is the subject of rumour only and there is no proof of what John Bellingham got up to. The story was that he became fascinated with the sea and wanted to go under sail. In April 1787, Uncle William negotiated with the owners of the *Hartwell*. They agreed to take on the young John, who at 15 was tall for his age. The reports say he was hired as a midshipman, but any records that list the midshipmen do not include his name. If he indeed did sail on the *Hartwell*, it would

John Bellingham in the Apprentices List.

more likely to have been in a minor role, perhaps cabin boy, as he could not boast of any experience on the sea. Whatever the case, the *Hartwell* sailed out of Gravesend with a very rich cargo, destined for China.

The voyage was to be quite an adventure as, whilst at sea, disputes arose between the crew and her captain, Edward Fiott. They crew felt a degree of injustice in their treatment and a letter of demands was presented to the captain. He spurned the demands and flogged the ringleaders, which led to an open mutiny which was put down with great violence. Unfortunately, the *Hartwell* ran onto rocks and the ship was lost. Most of the crew survived and Fiott and his chief mate were held responsible for the disaster and Fiott would later write a full account of the voyage. If John Bellingham had been on board, there are two things that echo in what would occur later. The sense of an injustice and belief of being wronged and harshly treated and the writing of a letter setting out complaints and seeking redress. Many seamen of that day were illiterate, whilst young Bellingham was very able with the pen. Could he have been asked to scribe the letter? Was this something he picked up and noted for his own use in the future?

We then have two reliable sources that place John Bellingham in Oxford Street, London in 1793. One of these was a trustee of Bellingham's father's will, writing later he gave the full details of Bellingham being set up in this business. It was an 'oil and tin-plate' concern, using what he had learned in Mr Love's shop. His mother's sparse resources once again are being used to indulge him and fund his

John Bellingham's final dividend announcement.

new enterprise. However, his abandonment of the apprenticeship had not allowed him to acquire the acumen needed to run a business and it was declared bankrupt in March 1794. The newspapers on 8 November 1796 declare the final dividend of the bankruptcy had been paid. Shortly after that, he was given his discharge papers and free to continue in business activity. There is also the record of Bellingham's conversation much later, in which he confirms that he indeed had the business in Oxford Street. Whilst in bankruptcy, Bellingham had recourse to his good education and his accountancy and writing skills. These allowed him to take employment in the Counting Houses in London and it was here that he got a taste for international trade. He was astute enough to realise that in the transactions he was dealing with, large sums were changing hands. He had had enough of failure, poverty and struggling and no doubt set his heart on making his own fortune.

Chapter 3

Marriage, Trading and Trouble

John Bellingham is a man who is hard to pin down from the records. If later statements from Mary Bellingham are correct, in about 1798 he had become associated with John Neville, a man involved in a similar trade to Bellingham and who was just as prone to bankruptcy. Mary was his daughter and she was born in County Armagh, Ireland, either at Newry or Lurgan. Bellingham, for reasons of love, or the opportunity for gain, married her in Ireland. The Trustee of Bellingham's father's will, claimed that 'he misrepresented his situation' when in Ireland. As we will see, this is very likely as we discover how Bellingham handled and saw the truth. No record of the marriage has been found anywhere in Irish or English records. The couple came over from Ireland and lived at Richmond Row in Liverpool.

There he 'acted as an agent for a Mr Dorbecker', a Dutch merchant who operated a Merchant House at Archangel in Russia, moving cargo between England, Russia, Sweden, Germany and Holland. His connection to Bellingham arises from his acting as an agent for William Osbourne, a Hull merchant, and James Neville, his father in law. Soon after he married, Bellingham was off to Archangel, taking Mary with him – perhaps his idea of a honeymoon. In 1801, according to census data, James Bellingham, his son, was born in Russia. Mary Bellingham would later give testimony that her husband 'left her at Archangel for nine months without any means of support'. Bellingham had abandoned his wife to her own devices and she said she had to 'rely on friends'. In all later accounts, Bellingham does not record this incident. Because of the timescale it does not appear to be related to the later event which would be at the heart of the story that would lead to his ultimate tragedy. The fact is that he had apparently gone to St Petersburg and from there to England:

> 'for the purpose of bringing home all papers and documents relating to Dorbecker's House, they having stated that he was a partner in the concern.'

There is no record of what it was that caused this need for Bellingham to return to England without Mary on this occasion. After this return, he was back in Russia until 1802. Things do not seem to have gone well with his arrangements with Dorbecker and, as we will see, this bodes ill for the future.

The family returned to Hull later that year. There we find Bellingham again with money problems and being pursued by people making claims upon him. His character appears either to be one of stupidity, craftiness or maybe he was simply a victim of misfortune. The one thing that emerges about Bellingham is that, with him, nothing appears straightforward. In a substantial document with attachments, Bellingham had a book printed, dated 1804, which was addressed to his 'agent' Mr Peter Ellis. He gave the booklet the title *Blunders or Statements of Facts*. It gives us his own account of what happened in Hull. It was a rather long and involved explanation of his time in Hull, again pleading that he was being mistreated and charged wrongly to owe money.

This book recorded that Bellingham set off from Hull for Hamburg on behalf of Dorbecker; the date is not given. Bellingham's account casts doubt on the clean-cut image often portrayed in other reports. He went into an inn in Hamburg and played cards and lost two shillings (£10). He, when laying out his case against his Hull creditors, wrote:

> 'You Hull gentlemen who wallow in opulence may be able to smile: but when it is known that this sum [lost in gambling] was as serious to me as if Mr Bankworth [One of his creditors] was to sustain a loss of £48,000 [£500,000], I hope you will readily compose your features, for it was four fifths of all I had in the world.'

If this were true, it shows both a reckless and foolish character, who risks the bulk of what money he has in a foreign country.

However, this is not the end to his foolishness. In the document he recounts another episode, this time in Bremen. Whether it is on the same visit or not, is not clear. This time he claims to have arrived in Bremen with £60. He then gave £50 to an innkeeper. Bellingham wrote:

> 'I landed at Bremen with £60 [£6,000] being inclined to pass a little time in the country, with a view to learn German, I banked £50 [£5,000] of my capital with one Smith, who was both a house-keeper, a countryman, and as I thought a friend, into whose hands I reposed it with confidence, being diffident of trusting myself with so large a sum.'

Bellingham had never met the man before and it is astounding that he entrusted such a sum to, a stranger. Mr Smith went back to England with Bellingham's money and £2,000 (£205,000) of other people's money. Four weeks later Bellingham returned to the inn and discovered his loss.

What transpired points to a certain craftiness within Bellingham. He discovered that the said Mr Smith was now being detained in custody back in England for bankruptcy so he therefore had no choice, with his lack of funds, but to stay at the inn. There a shoemaker, a man connected to the 'Count Quod of Garsthorpe near Wesel', arrived looking for Mr Smith; it appeared the Count owed him around $80 (£6,000). Bellingham introduced himself to the shoemaker and persuaded him to bring the money to him. The shoemaker obliged and brought back a bag of cash which Bellingham 'happily' made his own. Whilst other creditors were helping themselves to Mr Smith's meagre property, Bellingham had schemed to have the cream. It does not end there; Bellingham heard that Mr Smith had left a gold watch with a watchmaker for repair and he went to the shop to try and obtain it, as it 'presented a glorious opportunity to take care of myself'. His attempt to obtain the watch was thwarted, even when he hired a lawyer and went to the local Bench. Although he did later write to Smith telling him what he had done, the incident adds a side to Bellingham's character that has been missed in other accounts of his life.

He was not making a great deal of money from what the records suggest. However, he was still looking out for that main chance. We know from a letter he wrote that he was in Hull on 8 December 1802. The records indicate that early in 1803, he had returned to Archangel on his own behalf to arrange a shipment on board the ship *Atlas*, no doubt part funded by a legacy. He recorded that the ship was lost and it cost him £1,700 (£150,000). Indeed, Lloyds do have a record that the *Atlas* was driven ashore and wrecked at 'Sololilza' in 1803, with her crew being rescued. One of those merchants with whom he entered into a dispute told Bellingham that the loss of his investment was God's punishment on him for how he had conducted business.

In Archangel, Bellingham also acted as an adviser to Mr Nicholas Osbourne. On 30 August 1803, Osbourne wrote to Bellingham regarding a shipment from Archangel. This would become a source of dispute later. Osbourne again wrote from Archangel on 22 November 1803 to his father in Hull, stating he was 'much obliged to Mr John Bellingham who has done everything in his power in dispatching the ships at Onega [Archangel]'. It was on 6 Dec 1803 that Lloyds listed the loss of a ship called the *Sojus*. This too would be an issue for Bellingham on his next return to Russia.

Bellingham arrived back at Hull in early 1804, on board a shipped called the *Neptune*, on 28 April 1804. From the ship, Bellingham wrote to William Osbourne about a dispute that was brewing. He disembarked from the ship, straight into that troubled brew.

Chapter 4

The Sponging House and the Horse Tails

lunders or Statements of Facts records that Osbourne had a dispute with
Bellingham over what he claimed were Bellingham's recommendation of
Dorbecker, the Dutch merchant. It is to be noted that Bellingham made
clear in the document a number of times that he acted as an agent for Dorbecker,
an arrangement which provided him with an income. The particular deals at
dispute involved Osbourne agreeing a shipment of wood from Archangel to Hull
and the shipment of grain to an unspecified port from Archangel. On the wood
shipment, Dorbecker had a signed agreement between himself and Osbourne. This
should have been lodged with the Russian authorities at St Petersburg, however,
Dorbecker did not lodge it and the shipment was sold to another merchant. This
was one more thing that should have alerted Bellingham to Dorbecker's character
flaws. Osbourne's son, Nicholas, discovered this and subsequently his father lost
expected profit on the deal. The second shipment of grain could not be loaded on
a ship for on-forwarding, as it did not arrive at Archangel as expected. The reasons
given were that 'enemy activity' prevented it. Whatever the true reason, once again
Osbourne lost out on his profits. Bellingham made clear where his priorities lay in
the matter, throwing in a bit of Scripture:

> 'Good sometimes results from evil, and we both have been taught a lesson.
> You never more to truft [trust] a foreigner, and *me* [Bellingham's emphasis]
> never to neglect my own concerns to attend to those of other people.'

Osbourne insisted that Bellingham had given him confidence that Dorbecker was
honourable and trustworthy and so Bellingham was therefore liable for Osbourne's
losses. In a lengthy defence of his actions, Bellingham insists that he did no
such thing. He believed that Osbourne's decision to trust Dorbecker arose from
his [Osbourne's] association with James Neville and his own judgment. What is
notable is that when Bellingham sets out his argument he infuses it with Christian
quotations. He also resorts to the use of legal language and quoting of law.

Whilst Bellingham admitted to a discussion about Dorbecker, he resolutely
denied he ever gave any support to the character of Dorbecker or encouraged
Osbourne to do business with him. It has to be said that his denial stretches credulity.
Bellingham was Dorbecker's agent and would profit from any arrangements to

trade. Is it conceivable that Bellingham would not encourage business that would be to his profit? Had he also not been involved in some issues on his last visit to Archangel necessitating getting papers from England? Surely there is at least the case that an honest man would make any prospective victim aware of Dorbecker, knowing what he was. Indeed, Bellingham rather played the innocent abroad calling himself 'a stripling in mercantile'. If Osbourne had asked Bellingham 'as a friend', then Bellingham, the 'stripling', declared he would have advised caution and offers a piece of worldly wisdom:

> 'For a number of years it has been an indelible maxim with me, that caution is the mother of security, so that when a stake is large. It is judicious to play a safe game, instead of acting as Mr Osbourne did.'

It would appear that maxim did not apply in Bremen with Bellingham's gambling and trusting of Mr Smith. Furthermore, what does it say of his character that he obviously knew Dorbecker was untrustworthy and yet in conversation as 'a friend' or otherwise makes no mention of it?

Bellingham then asserted that Osbourne was not the only one Dorbecker misused, indeed he himself was a victim; 'Dorbecker has used me like a rascal, as he is.' Remarkably however, he went on to justify Dorbecker's actions in not supplying the grain, even asserting that, 'I profess, and indeed trust, I have a common share of common sense.' Bellingham's work and business history might suggest otherwise.

Then Bellingham appealed for sympathy:

> 'I am one who never possessed the advantage of many, in having a father before me and being destitute of a friend to give me a start in life; was obliged at a tender age and uneducated, to launch unprotected, into the world, and coped with severe difficulties and unexampled severities, of which I was but too sensible.'

This betrays Bellingham's character as a manipulator and indeed even a liar. It is true that the loss of a father is a tragic thing for a young boy. However, had not his mother gone to great lengths to cushion him? What about his uncle, the kindly William Daw? He had set him up in a very good apprenticeship at his own considerable expense. He ran away from that position at 15, hardly a 'tender' age in those days. As to being uneducated, it is very obvious that he wrote well, knew the Scriptures, could cite the law and indeed his expansive writing shows him very well equipped to protect himself – hardly a case for a poor education.

Osbourne went further in attacking Bellingham. He accused him (and Mary) of attempting to read his son Nicholas' private correspondence whilst in Russia. Furthermore, in Osbourne's account, Bellingham broke down a locked door to enter the son's room to see the letters. Osbourne gave the names of three ship captains who witnessed the incident. Bellingham dismissed the whole charge, claiming he spoke to one of the witnesses who denied seeing anything and the rest was mere hearsay. After a long defence of himself he in turn attacked Osbourne's son, quoting Scripture, 'He did the things he ought not to have done, and neglected the things which he ought to have done.' In this particular case, it seems the only thing at stake is Bellingham's reputation:

> 'I have been a warfarer [Bellingham's own term for warrior] in the world and alone obliged to fight its battles, from the incidents of my life have had to do with various classes of mankind, and when I have been insulted by the spurious dregs of the scum of society, I uniformly passed it off with contempt, imputing it to their ignorance; but when these things happen from men of sense, I ever felt the wound.'

No resolution on financial settlement is recorded. There was a letter written on 16 May 1812, to Thomas Thompson MP, from Oswald Smith, a businessman, of Hull who confirms the Hull incident and the debt owed to Osbourne. Bellingham shows arrogance and that aggressiveness as a 'warrior' that made him a man who could not let things go. His weapons were pen and paper, but as we will see, that would not always be the case.

The second matter was with a Mr Bankworth, a merchant at Hull and his partner Mr Dowson. They had entered into another deal with Dorbecker and a sum of £100 (£9,000) was in dispute. Bankworth wanted the whole £100, whereas Bellingham felt he was only due £12 7s 7d (£1,100). By the time of this dispute, Bellingham claimed to be no longer acting as an agent for Dorbecker.

Bellingham had not settled the account and was charged with being a debtor and was arrested and placed in the Myton Gate Sponging House at Hull. The Sponging House was a place of confinement for debtors; if anyone was charged with debt, the creditor laid a complaint with the sheriff, the sheriff sent his bailiffs, and the debtor would be taken to the Sponging House. This was not a prison but usually a private house, often the bailiff's own home. The debtor would be held there until payment was made or some other arrangement agreed with the creditors. If no agreement was made after a period of time, the debtor was moved to the local gaol. Bellingham was in the Sponging House on 3 May 1804 from where he wrote to Samuel Martin who is the attorney for Bankworth and Dowson, setting out his case.

Bellingham's meticulous accounting is then seen as he lays out his case in defence of the claim:

> 'The entire of Bankworth and Dowson's demand against Mr Dorbecker was £843 1s 3d [78,000]. Every farthing of which was paid, viz. £514 6s 6d in Mr Dorbecker's property.

..pr £328 14s 9d in my own.
The payment on my part was in a lot of goods,
----amounting to. £416 7s 2d
From which deduct £328 14s 9d
_____leave £87 12s 3d [£8,000]
my property which at the time I ought to have received.
[As laid out by Bellingham]'

The issue was that Bankworth felt he and his partner were due demurrage. Demurrage represents liquidated damages for delays and he had raised a bill against Bellingham for the £100. He accordingly set out his counter claim:

'Amount of bill _ _ _ £100. 0s 0d from which deduct balance left in their hands 87. 12. 5
12. 7. 7 due Messrs. Bankworth and Dowson
[As laid out by Bellingham]'

This shows that side of his character of keeping records and being detailed in his dealings with others, holding them to exact account.

He wrote his defiance in his not paying the bill:

'… which, if Mr Bankworth is not satisfied with, and insists on the £87 besides, I can say as the countryman did to Queen Elizabeth ; "Madam – you have got the wrong sow by the ear!"'

Not only does this suggest the stubbornness of Bellingham but his education. The remark he quotes was that of Queen Elizabeth I's aide who used it of some Italian architects who thought they could take the queen for a fool. No uneducated man would know that detail.

The result of his defiance was that two days later he was moved to the Hull prison. From here he wrote to a 'friend' stating that he had been found 'inflexible, in intending to contend the suit' and the Sponging House owner, Mr Mason, 'supposed there was no probability of my procuring bail'. Then in a phrase that will return in similar terms in the future, he bemoaned his being hard done by:

'It is the wish of my adversaries to hamper and harass me as much as possible, but it won't do; feeling as happy where I am, in my own breast, as if at perfect liberty; the terrors of the law and the shame of a gaol do not extend to the innocent, and consequently, have no hold on me, therefore I defy the world to do its worse.'

He continued to claim injustice and being misunderstood and a victim - a common theme with Bellingham. He asked his 'friend' to recommend a good lawyer.

On the 10 May 1804, he was still in jail and picked up his pen once more to do battle, this time with the sub-Sherriff of the town of Hull who also happened to be Samuel Martin, the lawyer of the plaintiff Bankworth, his creditor. There are no niceties in the opening address, rather an all-out attack on the recipient, hardly the way to win friends:

> 'Malice may do its worse, and unprincipled avarice its grasp, till it foams and fritters and perseveres in nothing but wrong, and meanness; for little actions are the unerring symbols of little minds; but when a man who is clothed with a high official office, and placed as a guardian of justice, I say, that man, when instead of being the father, becomes the violator of the laws; how much is he not to be despised, and how necessary to be made an example of; but the day of restitution is at hand.'

His introduction in this letter shows us a man who holds a black and white view of 'justice'. He felt he was being treated unfairly and therefore believes retribution is justified. A foreboding of what is to come.

Bellingham in his letter was no longer addressing the debt. Rather he was now claiming that his detention was illegal. This again will echo in his future. Bellingham once more shows himself as the 'lawyer'. He wrote that Martin should know the warrant for Bellingham's arrest was 'illegal'. If Martin did not know, then he was 'ignorant'. If he did know then he was 'ten times worse'. He contended that this sort of thing 'is too frequent' and that it is dangerous to the one who is subject to it. For this kind of illegal detention, there is a fine to be paid to the king. He therefore threatened to 'make a motion to the King's Bench with a view to levy a fine'. Again, as we will see, this was a typical action of Bellingham, appealing to the highest possible authority. In doing this he would:

> '... prove, that if neither of you, or Mr Bankworth are lovers of justice,
> I am, although a prisoner, and thereby evince in the world, that it is
> principle, and not place, that constitutes a rogue.'

In case Martin is 'ignorant' of the law, Bellingham added a PS to explain that Martin in signing the warrant for arrest, whilst being the lawyer of the creditor, acted illegally. Bellingham claimed he was an 'ignoramus' to this illegality and became aware of it 'accidently' from 'a brother in limbo'. There is no record of anyone visiting Bellingham, so it is likely a fellow prisoner was the 'brother'. Bellingham expanded on this legal statement to his agent Peter Ellis. In this he quoted chapter and verse of the law showing that on release he had made a point of tracing the exact wording of the statute, once more revealing something of his pedant nature. He wrote;

'The under-sheriff performs all the duties of the office, except when the personal presence of the High Sheriff is necessary. But he shall not abide in his office above one year, 42 Edw. III. C.9-23 Hen. VI. C.8, forfeits £200 [£18,000 2017]. He shall not practice as an attorney during the time he continues in such office; it would be a great inlet to partiality and oppression [Bellingham's quotation marks].'

Indeed, it appears there was a miscarriage of justice, if only in the arrest, and this only caused bitterness to grow in Bellingham against 'these villains', a bitterness that would later bear terrible fruit.

After writing to Martin, Bellingham picked up his pen again on the same day, without a recipient, calling it 'Amusement in Prison'. In many ways, it is indeed amusing. The letter started with a reprise of the demurrage issue with Bankworth and then went on to recount the incident of the horse tails. When Bellingham had been in Russia he had manged to buy a consignment of horse tails and brought them back to Hull just before Bankworth raised his claim for demurrage. When Bankworth heard of the horse tails, he thought he could make a quick profit. Bellingham set out in great detail how horse tails were traded. It seems that they are tied into bundles. The bundles are tied at both ends. If both ends are the same thickness then the tails are good and can sell for a handsome price. If they are thick at one end and thin at the other, they are of inferior quality.

They also come in various lengths, in this case twenty-four inches. Bellingham's tails were sold in a deal with Bankworth with Bellingham only telling him the length. An intricate deal involving percentage profits, was struck for 2s 6d (£10) per pound weight, with Bankworth, whom Bellingham described as, 'a novice'. Unfortunately, the tails were of the inferior quality and only sold for 9d (£3.50) per pound so Bankworth lost out in the deal. Bellingham found this amusing as he had all the signed documents showing that the trade was above board and 'one should have thought this was obvious to a child; but it never occurred to Bankworth'. It may well be that it was this trade that was at the bottom of the debt action against Bellingham, but it does also demonstrate a side to Bellingham's character that is not as honest as he would like to have portrayed to the world. He ends his complaint against his creditors stating of them:

'This is Mr Bankworth, who from my services in the Onega [Archangel] business, and my friendship regarding the Cornwallis, Captain Gordon, must in course of a few months have cleared little less than £2,000 [£205,000].'

The tone of Bellingham is one of bitter envy.

It appears from Bellingham's documents that some 'friends' came and raised bail for him. This is particularly puzzling in that Bellingham, in his note to Peter Ellis, talks of Bankworth being a £40,000 to £60,000 'man'. That would value Bankworth around £4 million pounds in 2017. Bellingham makes the claim 'I cannot boast of being worth more than a third of Mr Bankworth's property'. In modern terms, a millionaire. This cannot be the case as Bellingham continually struggled to make money and could not afford to pay the debt. It seems like an idle brag or more probably wishful thinking. However, there is one final twist to this; the *Hull Advertiser* in May printed an announcement that 'The debtors of Hull Gaol returned thanks to Mr Bellingham of Archangel for his kind donation of one guinea [£90]'. No matter who paid the guinea, perhaps it was for the legal advice he received from one of his fellow debtors.

Chapter 5

The Leaving of Liverpool for Archangel

After writing his pamphlet on the Hull period Bellingham moved to Liverpool. He published an advert to distribute among his 'friends', looking for new business. It would appear he was looking at getting involved in a company that was very prosperous, the White Sea Fishing Company which operated out of Archangel and coordinated the activities of Russian trappers. Involvement in such a lucrative trade would have been very attractive to Bellingham. He was also again interested in the wood trade that was flourishing at Archangel. The tone of the pamphlet suggests that Bellingham was setting himself up as an authority on the trade, with 'valuable Russian manuscripts that have fell into my hands'. One wonders how they 'fell' into his hands. It is also clear from Hull that he was in desperate need of funds and he was once more relying on getting a big money opportunity, rather than applying himself to a role in a Counting House with steady income. One could either admire Bellingham for his efforts to aspire in business or one could consider his business acumen as displayed to date, and consider him reckless and unwise. He had a wife and a 2-year-old son to consider. However, the next thing that Bellingham did was to charter a ship and head for Archangel to buy iron. On this enterprise Bellingham took his wife and young son and all three of them set sail from Liverpool around June 1804. June is a pleasant time to sail to Russia before the ice of winter. On arrival in Archangel they would have found the port a busy place, with a great deal of shipping activity with everyone in a hurry to avoid the ice.

Archangel was founded as a port in 1584 and thrived at the centre of the import/export trade for Russia. With the development of

John Bellingham in the Apprentices List.

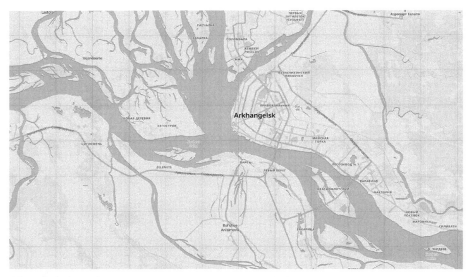

Map of Archangel.

St Petersburg in the early 1700s as the main port, Archangel declined, yet by 1803 was still able to be an important centre for trade. Sitting on the Northern Dvina River which empties itself into the White Sea, the port would become frozen in winter and be completely iced in for months. British companies who traded out of Archangel would bid for cargoes of wood, iron, fur, hemp etc. to feed the markets of Britain and Europe. They would hire a ship and place insurance cover with Lloyds in London and hope that the hazardous journey would be safely navigated and their profits brought home. In 1804, there was the constant danger of Privateers or enemy ships, attacking vessels flying the Union Jack. The routes of all ships heading to and from Archangel were carefully planned to avoid main areas of conflict. It was a risky business.

However, the merchants also needed to have an agent present in the port to ensure the tricky negotiations that surrounded the trade were carried out efficiently and with minimum costs. This would be the role of men like Bellingham who would either be employed by the buyer or who would act for commissions based on the value of the cargo. Bellingham on this journey was acting in the latter capacity.

On arrival at Archangel, he set about his intended business. What happened next is astounding. In the Hull debacle, we noted Bellingham was aware of Conrad Dorbecker's character. Had he not written, 'Dorbecker has used me like a rascal, as he is'? Yet when Bellingham is required to purchase a consignment of iron, he employed Dorbecker as agent to obtain it. He paid Dorbecker £500 (£45,000) to make the purchase from Solomon van Brienen, a merchant and a fellow Dutchman. The iron arrived at the port and was loaded onto vessels for England. Bellingham would later state that he had 'dispatched his vessels' and would presumably look

Artist's impression of St Petersburg c.1847 Vasily Sadovnikov.

forward to going home to enjoy his commission for the work. However, the 'rascal' Dorbecker had not paid for the iron and had become bankrupt. Van Brienen therefore looked to Bellingham as the purchaser of the iron to make good the default of his agent Dorbecker. The dispatch of the iron meant that the cargo could not be returned to the sellers.

Two things need to be noted here. Firstly, the foolish trait in Bellingham's character seen at Bremen in giving his money to a stranger is seen here again. Having been duped by Dorbecker once, it was sheer folly to trust him again. Secondly, Bellingham considered himself a just and honourable man. Therefore, as the purchaser of the iron from van Brienen, it was right and proper that he took responsibility for his agent's actions. We do not have any record from independent sources as to what actually happened at Archangel. We have only Bellingham's account and later statements from Government officials who were at St Petersburg and dealt with him in the aftermath of the dispute.

Mary Bellingham would confirm that arbitration had been entered into with a Mr Barker (a captain in the East Middlesex Militia) as the arbitrator along with three others. However, the result was that 'Mr Bellingham was imprisoned in Archangel'. Mary tells us something also missing from all Bellingham's accounts of this time. She records that:

THE RIGHT HONOURABLE
LORD GRANVILLE LEVESON GOWER.
From an original Picture by T. PHILLIPS, ESQ. R.A. *in the Possession of the*
RIGHT HON: LORD HOLLAND.
Drawn by J. Wright. Engraved by J. S. Agar.

PUBLISHED MOTT, HELET, T. CADELL & W. DAVIES, STRAND, LONDON.

An engraving of Lord Leveson Gower.

'he [her husband] sent her with her brother to St Petersburg to lay all the papers before Sir Stephen Shairp and Lord Leveson Gower and from whom he expected redress.'

She noted that they informed her that they could 'not render any assistance'.

Sir Stephen Shairp, the Secretary to Lord Gower British Ambassador in Archangel, would confirm the arbitration as he later acted to investigate Bellingham's claim, with the Governor General of Archangel and they were:

'... referred for decision to four merchants, two British merchants being appointed on the part of Bellingham, and two other persons on the part of Dorbecker. By the award of those arbitrators, Bellingham was declared to be indebted to the assignees of Dorbecker the sum of two thousand roubles'

However, before that investigation took place, van Brienen, brought a claim against Bellingham in the court at Archangel. The affidavit was issued against Bellingham who had climbed on board a carriage on 15 November 1804, to go to St Petersburg to depart by ship to England with Mary and his son. Bellingham dramatizes the event, writing in the third person, 'he was seized, dragged out of his Kabitky [A Russian carriage] and thrown into Prison'. Whilst Bellingham went to prison, his wife and son travelled on to St Petersburg.

An alternative narrative has been suggested as to the purchase of the iron – that it never was made. It is suggested that the two Dutchmen conspired together to defraud the Englishman and that the claim for the money was bogus. This version does have problems. Firstly, Bellingham himself, as noted already, said he had dispatched the vessels, presumably with cargo that had been 'purchased'. Secondly, Lord Gower's secretary, in recounting the arbitration, noted that the two parties were Bellingham and 'the house of Dorbecker' who had raised a counter-claim against Bellingham. The four business men appointed to look into the matter – and two of them were on Bellingham's side – decided in Dorbecker's favour. It would suggest that they had seen evidence that justified the claim against Bellingham.

By now the port of Archangel had iced over and the harsh winter conditions settled on the port. Bellingham was languishing in the prison and sending requests for his release to the General Governor, the Magistrates and to Lord Gower and his Secretary, Stephen Shairp. The latter wrote to the Governor of Archangel to make a case for the release of Bellingham 'if not legally detained'. In response, the Governor replied that Bellingham had 'behaved very indecorously, and that he was legally detained'.

On 23 January 1805, Bellingham wrote to the Governor General stating clearly his rejection of the claims made upon him. This was followed with another letter in early February complaining of his not being able to go to St Petersburg. 10 February brought another letter to the Governor General setting out his grievance against Popov, the Mayor of Archangel, and Dorbecker and once more claiming illegal detention. On 4 March, Bellingham was again writing to the Governor that his 'trunk' has been seized and taken away by the magistrate. He continued to express his indignation and innocence and with force writes, 'I both hope and expect an immediate order for my liberation.' This letter shows Bellingham's increasing indignation and frustration at his treatment. 5 March found Bellingham writing again expressing disappointment that he had not had an answer from the Governor. His growing impatience was obvious and once more he claimed that all charges were 'falsehoods' and his detention 'illegal'. 26 March brought another letter and this time, whilst there is pathos in the writing, there is also still that aggression. He stated that he had written to the Governor 'requesting his immediate release' and had no response. Bellingham wanted to know 'how much longer it is your Excellency's pleasure for me to continue' in his situation.

In the next communication on 12 May, Bellingham was angry. He complained that the Governor had written a letter to Shairp 'stating that my behaviour has been highly indecorous'. Bellingham 'must therefore take the liberty of saying' that 'the word of a General Governor ought to be sacred'. He further wrote that he 'cannot refrain from astonishment' at what was written by the Governor. However, Bellingham did admit to having 'acted a little vociferous' but excused this because of his circumstances. Furthermore, he went on to accuse the Governor of lying. He insisted the Governor had agreed that the claimants against Bellingham 'had gone beyond the Law'. However, the Governor was now denying that. Bellingham wrote, 'These truths which your own conscience must confirm, and though disacknowledged, yet the facts remain.'

This series of letters once more points to Bellingham's character. He is convinced of his own truth in a situation. There is no movement from him or any chance of him misunderstanding the events. There is no possibility in Bellingham's mind of his not achieving his aim, in this case release and compensation. This dogged inflexibility will now drive him more than ever towards his final action to seek redress. The Governor was totally unmoved by Bellingham and he remained in his prison.

There is also a letter that Lord Gower wrote to Bellingham on 6 May 1805 acknowledging Bellingham's letters. Gower wrote, 'I have received your several letters up to 31 March inclusive.' The letter continued with Gower expressing regret at Bellingham's detention in Archangel, but he stated that he could not intervene because of the Governor General's letter to Shairp. Gower further wrote:

> 'At the same time, however that I say this, I wish you to understand, that provided you can furnish me with such evidence of your having been unjustly used, as will authorise my interference on this subject, I shall very readily take such steps on your behalf.'

Bearing in mind the political atmosphere, with the Napoleonic war that was raging and relations between Britain and Russia very delicate, British representatives in Russia had to tread carefully. Shairp also informed Bellingham that he needed to produce proof that the Governor of Archangel was wrong. What more could Shairp and Gower do?

The situation became complicated by a further claim. Van Brienen and 'Mr Popoff' (as spelt by Bellingham but more likely to be Popov) were co-owners of a Ship called the *Sojus*. The Lloyd's List dated Tuesday, 6 December 1803 records the shipping activity in the previous week and it had the short note, '*Sojus*, from Archangel, is lost near Sololiza; crew saved'. It was alleged that the owners had attempted a fraud on Lloyds for losses connected with the ship and van Brienen charged with perjury and no compensation was paid. Van Brienen in turn accused Bellingham of being the anonymous informant to Lloyds and responsible for their losses connected with the ship. They therefore instituted criminal proceedings against him. Inquiries made in London, by whom we do not know, apparently cleared Bellingham of this charge, though we have only Bellingham's account of this.

Following this, he claims that the *Procureur* (court official) of Archangel wrote a report to the Minister of Justice at St Petersburg which he quoted from, that he (Bellingham) 'was extremely ill-used, and that he was illegally detained'. Bellingham further stated, 'it appeared afterwards that Sir Stephen Shairp read the said report at Price Lapuchin's, the Minister of Justice.' However, according to Bellingham, nothing was done about the report for six months and only then would he be freed by the Governor General of Archangel. Lord Gower would later write of this situation but made no mention of Shairp seeing a report. Gower recorded later in 1812, 'he was taken to prison; but was soon after liberated, in consequence, I believe, of a second application to the Governor from Sir Stephen Shairp.'

However, by October 1805, Bellingham was still held in Archangel. Having exhausted his correspondence with the Governor, he now turned to the *Graschdanskaja Palata*, the State Court. In a very long petition of sixteen clauses, we again get a glimpse into Bellingham's character. In the opening clause, he accepted that if there is an account to be settled then he would settle it, if the claimants would issue an invoice. He went on to state that he believed they could not do this because there was no claim. His dignity and pride is an obvious issue for Bellingham and he recounted the 'violence' of his arrest. Furthermore, the seizing of his 'Portmanteau' and the reading of his 'private letters' along with their searching through his books and other items of clothing added to his distress.

Once again, he displayed some understanding of the law and his rights and the effrontery at the injustice of his detention, arguing that in all this searching nothing was ever found to substantiate the claims against him. Having experienced indignities and been questioned, he now insisted that the claimants be questioned under oath. He then made the case that an arbiter had found him 'ill-used' but yet went on to question their honesty and integrity when they declared he had a case to answer. He then claimed that the *Procureur* had judged him to be 'ill-used and illegally detained'. The use by Bellingham of the term 'ill-used' occurs very regularly in his writings when describing how others have treated him. This is important in understanding his later actions. Throughout his life he is often found to be in financial difficulties with claims against him. He always appears to be a man looking for a fortune but never finding it. The reason, it would seem from his writings, is that in his mind, his failures are due to being ill-used. We never find any record that suggests any of his failures were his own responsibility. This in turn caused Bellingham to claim a sense of injustice, a sense that drove him to never give up in pursuit of what he believed he deserved, whether that belief was rooted in reality or not.

This part of Bellingham's story therefore tells us of his character and reinforces the trait of his doggedness in his pursuit of what he sees as justice. In the time of his imprisonment at Archangel, he wrote an amazing number of letters and made many applications to the courts. He was completely blinkered in his belief of his own righteousness in the matter. The later petition we have in which he outlined his version of events does not mention anywhere the investigation that was undertaken by the four businessmen to ascertain the truth and their findings. Neither did he mention the claims from Dorbecker against him. Finally, he gave no acknowledgement to Shairp for his part in attempting to get him released. He wrote to the police:

> 'I was surrounded by enemies; but he [Baron Asch the new Civil Governor of Archangel who replaced Governor General Furster who had been dealing with Bellingham] generously stepped forward, and bringing the matter into a Court of Justice. I obtained judgment against the whole party, including the Military Governor who had injured me.'

There are no other papers that confirm Bellingham's account. What was available suggests that the claims on the *Sojus* had been discounted and the new Governor wanted rid of an irritant. It appears that Bellingham was displaying a character trait in which he interprets events to his own credit. As we have seen before in him, there was a belief that the world was against him and he bore no responsibility for his situation. In the Hull dispute, he evoked the image of the poor fatherless boy, who was adrift in a world and no one cared for him, totally ignoring those around him who had helped and whom he had let down. In Archangel, the help from Shairp and the offer of help from Lord Gower was also totally ignored. For Bellingham, there was only one side to the story and that was his.

Chapter 6

Archangel to St Petersburg

Bellingham was released and there was no independent explanation as to why. On 18 October he wrote:

> 'The Assignees of Mr Dorbecker not having established their claims as required by Law after a complete investigation of the affair in the Dooma – the obligation I gave on the 6th Sept is entirely done away – and moreover the Procureur has reported that I have been illegally detained. Therefore it is to give notice that I purpose parting for St Petersburg in a few days unless legal cause is shown to the contrary in writing, notice of which have also been given to His Excellency the Governor General & Procureur.'

Without any documentation of an account from Russia we can only speculate as to the true reasons Bellingham was not prevented from leaving Archangel. The fact is that he was not only refusing to pay, but is highly likely that that he had no money to settle any claims against him. It therefore was probably an expedient measure, facilitated by Shairp's intervention, as stated by Lord Gower. Whatever the reason, Bellingham now made the journey to St Petersburg to join his wife and presumably would be expected to head back to Liverpool.

It was early November in 1805 when Bellingham arrived in St Petersburg. The city was the imperial capital of Russia and a major centre of trade with a port to send and receive goods to and from every corner of the world. On arrival in St Petersburg, Bellingham would have gone immediately to see his wife Mary and their young son. What joy there must have been on seeing his family after his confinement in the cold damp conditions of Archangel. Mary would have been overjoyed, having had to cope alone in the large city for so long. She would now want the family to return to their home in Liverpool and put the bad experience of Russia behind them. Any sensible man, having spent six months in a damp, cold prison, would surely have the same concern himself. Getting his wife and his baby son out of a country that had proved so unfriendly would be the priority.

What does it say about Bellingham's character and mental state, that he does not do this? Incredibly he puts his 'injured reputation' first. He decided to impeach General Furster, the Military Governor of Archangel, to the new Justice Minister, Count Kotzebue. Once again, he demonstrates the pedantic approach to such matters. He sets out three reasons:

'First. For having sanctioned Mr Solomon Van Brienen in an improper Oath, knowing it to be so

'Second. For having written an untrue account of the affair to Sir Stephen Shairp, His Majesty's Counsel, for the purpose of preventing justice

'Third. For causing him [Bellingham] to be thrown into a loathsome Military Prison for the purpose of extorting from him a sum of money with a view to colour the transaction and thereby pave the way for a justification of his own conduct and that of others.'

As we examine Bellingham's character in these statements, we find his belief that his reputation had been injured blinded him to common sense. The documents show a sequence of events. Van Brienen made the claim against Bellingham/Dorbecker. Dorbecker in turn, being bankrupt, passed the blame to Bellingham, the buyer. The four business men examined the case and found against Bellingham. Van Brienen then raised the issue of the *Sojus* and made his oath against Bellingham. Then enquiries were made at London. Archangel is iced in and so a message to London would have to go through another port. That could take at least six months and probably explains why Bellingham was held for that time. General Furster would have to accept van Brienen's claim until proven otherwise, therefore the acceptance of the oath was valid.

Whether Van Brienen made a false oath is a different matter. When the General then made his report to Shairp, he could only report what he found. Lord Gower's letter is helpful here:

'I remember that immediately upon the receipt of this letter [from Bellingham], I consulted with Sir Stephen Shairp, who agreed not only to write a letter to the Governor-General, requiring an explanation of the circumstances of which Bellingham complained, but also to his own mercantile correspondents, British residents at Archangel, for their opinion of the conduct of the Russian Government towards the complainant. It appeared from these inquiries, that Bellingham having been engaged in commercial business with the house of J Dorbecker and Co. pecuniary claims were made by each party against the other, and that these claims had been, by the Governor-General, referred for decision to four merchants, two British merchants being appointed on the part of Bellingham, and two other persons on the part of Dorbecker. By the award of those arbitrators, Bellingham was declared to be indebted to the assignees of Dorbecker the sum of two thousand roubles. This sum Bellingham, notwithstanding this decision, refused to pay. It also appeared from the communications received from Archangel, that a criminal suit had been instituted against Bellingham, by the owners of a Russian ship which had been lost in the White Sea

They accused him of having written an anonymous letter that had been received by the Underwriters in London, in which letter it was stated that the insurance of that ship was a fraudulent transaction; and payment for the loss of her had been in consequence resisted. No satisfactory proof was adduced against Bellingham, and he was acquitted of this charge.'

Once again, Bellingham ignored his own behaviour of acting 'indecorously' in charging the general of bad conduct. If we accept the word 'indecorously' as carefully chosen, we see an echo of the charges made against Bellingham in Hull towards Nicholas Osbourne. It seems Bellingham lost all sense of proportion when confronted by others who see things different from himself, reacting badly. This will not be the last time he will do so.

Bellingham was not only seeking justification of his supposedly good character, he also wanted compensation. We have to bear in mind that Bellingham knew Russia. He has demonstrated a working knowledge of the Law. He would be aware that, at this time in history, conditions in Russia for Englishmen had deteriorated and that Russian authorities were reluctant to offer any support to them. In perspective, Bellingham was an unknown. He had no rank or significance of any kind in the eyes of the powerful in Russia. He was simply one of the many Englishmen who had come to Russia to exploit her and make their fortunes. Therefore, his decision to impeach a Russian Governor General was the height of folly. As we look at Bellingham's character we are again seeing a reckless foolishness, a man who is blind to reality and the plight of those around him; his wife Mary and his son. It appears his reputation and money were of the greatest importance to him.

The result of his attack on the Governor General was as would be expected in the circumstances. The Russian Senate issued a criminal *Ukase* (order) on the 5 June 1806 for the detention of Bellingham for having 'quitted Archangel in a clandestine manner'. There was also a civil charge for a debt of 'two thousand Rubbles'. The creditors at Archangel, despite Bellingham's belief, had not gone away. When Bellingham received the order to appear before the Court, he 'naturally concluded' it was to affirm his case for damages. He believed that the Governor General of Archangel had given 'answer to the allegations given against him with his vindication thereof'.

He continued, 'however, to my unspeakable surprise it did not take the least notice of those important points of law and natural justice.' In this we see a foretaste of Bellingham's approach. In his feeling of injury, law and natural justice should support him. If it does not then he will push his case to the limit of the law, and beyond. It appears Bellingham had left Archangel but Archangel remained determined to hunt Bellingham. On the 11 June 1806, he was taken into detention by the city police to the High Court of justice at St Petersburg. He remained there whilst evidence was requested from Archangel; the report from there confirmed that Bellingham had in fact had a legitimate pass to leave the city and therefore no criminal charge could be made. This charge was therefore dismissed.

However, the civil claim remained in force and on 20 July 1806 Bellingham was transferred to the city prison in St Petersburg. He would later write:

> '… to my great surprise I was committed to the Thurm [City Jail] for the aforementioned pretended debt of 2000 roobles although they had received and it was then in their possession, the most indubitable voucher that I was not so much as in account with the parties to which the money was ordered to be paid.'

The *Ukase* from the Russian senate was very clear in its decision. They stated:

> '… a claim upon him [Bellingham] of 2000R for the benefit of the estate of the merchant Dorbecker at Archangel – afterwards on the 2nd October of the same year he was conveyed with the affair pending in that Court of Justice to the aforesaid College of Commerce – this college has enacted – as it has been ordered by the Senate's *Ukase* – to demand payment of the aforesaid money from Bellingham and on account of the non-payment of this sum Mr Bellingham is detained in the said College.'

This was not the only decision the Senate had made. The College had reported that Bellingham had declared that he had no money. Furthermore, he had stated that all his property was in England but he would not give the College any information or details of what that property was:

> 'The College is therefore of the opinion that according to the Bankrupt Laws (3 Sec 6 Ant,) in the event of the money not being paid within a month to announce him Bellingham to be a Bankrupt.'

They went on to state that Bellingham would be declared a bankrupt and would be sent to the city prison if he remained in default. Bellingham displays his complete blinkered approach to the Russian authorities. He could only see his damaged reputation and therefore someone should pay. Whatever the rights or wrongs of his case, he surely knew there was no chance whatsoever of getting settlement in his favour. His obstinacy saw him brought before the High Criminal Court on 27 August 1806 to explain why he had not paid his debts.

As we continue this portrait of Bellingham, let us remember where he now stood. He had been held in prison at Archangel for a disputed debt. Every avenue he tried to avoid payment, because he felt it unjust, was closed. Four businessmen, with two acting on his side, had looked at the matter and found against him. The initial *Ukase* made it

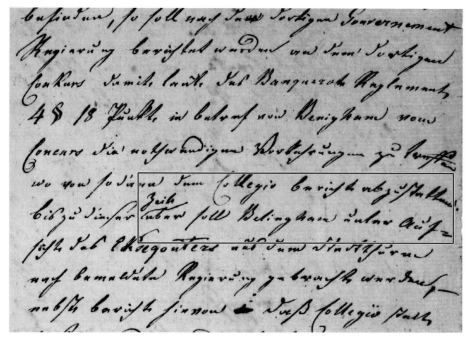

Portion of the document sent by the Russian College of Commerce to Bellingham confirming his liability for the debt.

clear there was still an issue over the debt. Then there was another rather important matter that had entered the picture; Mary was now pregnant with his second child and Bellingham again demonstrated his obstinate and destructive character. Instead of looking to the interests of his wife, son and unborn child, living in a hostile country and making them the priority, he stood on his perceived injured reputation. When called before the High Criminal Court he had the opportunity to accept the situation and reduced claim and get out of Russia. Indeed, a wiser man would have quit Russia with his wife and child and left the experience behind as a life lesson.

Furthermore, Bellingham had written to Alexander Shairp, the brother of the Secretary to Lord Gower, asking for financial aid. He replied to Bellingham on 6 September 1806 with a sympathetic but very direct letter. He advised Bellingham that any support he could raise would be a 'pittance'. Alexander continued:

'I must however observe to you that your behaviour is so unaccountable strange & so inconsistent with all reason that however willing people are to assist you it cannot be done without expugnance. [A classical reference to destruction] You fly in the face of your friends and tho' you ask of advice from the Minister and Counsul you are at the same time not inclined to follow what they [advised] you.'

Here Bellingham has been confronted with the truth and a very direct comment on his destructive behaviour. In the letter, he is further advised to accept that the legal process has given a decision and in order to extricate himself he should settle it. This was very wise advice. However, when he again appears before the Court he ignores it:

> 'I do not owe it, but if I do owe it, it is all the same to me to whom the money is paid – therefore if the *Palata* [The High Court] will have the goodness to produce a proper document on which it is demanded I would settle that instantly.'

He believed that what he said was 'simple and rational'. However, the Court did not agree and saw his tone as disrespectful of the Court and had him taken back to prison, with a three-day bread and water punishment.

Bellingham insisted, though, that it was because he would not pay the debt. His account of his time in prison is one of enduring great hardships. On 1 October 1806, he was moved to the College of Commerce. He would later set out his time in prison in a very detailed manner:

> 'In *Dooma* at Archangel 2 frm 3 to 5 March 1805
> " *Hauptwache* [Main Guard Building] 185 " 5 March to 6 Sept
> " *Gubarnsky Pralenia*
> " *Hoffgerichte S PBg* 40 " 11 June " 20 July 1806
> " *Thrum* 73 " 20 July " 1 Oct Do
> " *Gubarnsky Pralenia* 1" 1 Oct " 2 Oct Do
> " College of Commerce " 2 Oct to present date [1 March 1807]'

This is typical of Bellingham's nature; not only did he maintain an emotional and mental note of the wrongs, real or imagined, he invariably would record in detail the facts and figures.

Whatever thoughts there are on Bellingham's character, there is also the need to consider the conditions under which he was detained. He complained frequently of 'illegal treatment'. In this he was confined often in 'dungeons' and in a 'wretched loathsome Prison', fed on bread and water for days. As with other Russian prisoners, he would be moved from one location to another, often with a group of criminal felons. These movements would often attract attention from passers-by who, on occasions, would throw stones or refuse at prisoners. The conditions within Russian prisons at that time were foul. In certain locations, there would sometimes be a shortage of beds and prisoners would often sleep in shifts. Friedrich-Josef Haass, a doctor attending prisons in Russia from 1805, continually attempted to reform these conditions. He wrote of them:

'To this day the cells are dirty and the only toilet is a bucket, hygiene is lacking and the cells are so crowded that the prisoners have to sleep in shifts … We were called an island of mercy in a sea of cruelty; the cruelty was not only against those incarcerated, but also against those who sought to protect them.'

We can only imagine how Bellingham felt in such conditions. Any injustices he believed were inflicted upon him would be reinforced and driven deeper into his soul to fester and grow into an angry resentment as he sat among the filth of his imprisonment.

So it was that Bellingham was held at the College of Commerce in St Petersburg. This was a tribunal that considered commercial disputes involving English subjects and was agreed under a commercial treaty between Russia and Britain. From October 1806 to around the beginning of February 1807, Bellingham could not leave his place of confinement but then he was allowed to go for walks through the street. However, this was not freedom as he was always accompanied by a Police Officer.

It was on 1 March 1807 that a memorandum was sent by Bellingham to the Marquis of Douglas (Alexander Hamilton Douglas), who was the British Ambassador to Russia at that time. In the memorandum, he again outlined his claims of innocence and injustice. He asked that intervention be made to the Russian authorities for the claims against him to be dismissed and the College to release him; the Ambassador did not reply. Commenting on this, Bellingham now saw his treatment as an 'indignity to the Nation'. The non-reply of the Ambassador once more must have caused further anger and bitterness to grow in Bellingham. The great frustrations of continually being told he had no case to refuse to pay a debt he believed was not justified, were leading onwards to a fateful reckoning. One thing in his memorial to Douglas, is Bellingham's claim not to know to whom the debt was payable. This is not credible, as he had been informed in Archangel and in the *Ukase* that Dorbecker was the plaintiff.

By now, the pregnant Mary and her young son had returned to England through the charity of some unknown businessmen in St Petersburg. She had survived on earnings from her millinery and dress-making skills, always in the hope that her husband would return soon and take them home. Her patience must have given out and her concern was that her second child should not be born in Russia. At the end of May, Bellingham is once more writing. This time he has called in the Reverend Benjamin Beresford who acted as the Minister for British subjects in St Petersburg. This was to witness a sworn statement by him. It would be also witnessed by Alexander Shairp, on 1 June 1807.

The statement is a long account of Bellingham's difficulties to date, detailing the claims against him and his refutation of them. He listed his trials and tribulations and his feelings of indignity at his treatment. He included copies of his note to the police at Archangel regarding his leaving for St Petersburg along with the memorial to Douglas. There is a continual refrain that what was happening to him was against 'natural justice' and 'illegal'. He was adamant that action needed to be taken to free him and restore him with no stain on his character. He made it known that he had written to those who should have done better and ends, 'I have been the unfortunate personal sufferer'. There is a pathos in this ending and gives a glimpse into Bellingham's state of mind. Somehow, he believed that a sworn statement will effect what all his appearances before Courts and tribunals had failed to do – release him and pay him compensation. He has taken all the events, claims and rejections as very personal and his continual writings and pleas have had no avail. This statement would make no difference.

Whilst Bellingham was free to move around the city he was, as noted, at all times escorted by a Police Officer. Often, he would visit the home and office of Lord Gower, where Sir Stephen Shairp would give him money to support him in his captivity. On one outing at the end of July 1807, he decided to try and make a break for freedom and sanctuary. He fled from his guard and ran into the house of Lord Gower in St Petersburg, this time he wanted to remain whilst the British representatives arranged his release. Lord Gower allowed him to remain for one night. Gower described what happened in a later letter to Lord Castlereagh, the Foreign Secretary. In his letter, Gower made it clear that he was powerless to intervene in a matter determined by a Russian Court. However, he did also speak to the Minister for Foreign Affairs asking for the release of Bellingham as there 'was no prospect of recovering the sum of money required from him'. On 30 July 1807, Lord Gower wrote to Bellingham formally. He made it clear that under the circumstances he could not protect him 'from the custody of the Police Officer who accompanied' him. He went on:

> 'I must therefore request you give yourself up again into his custody but shall think it my duty to make representation to the Government upon your affairs & shall be happy to use any means in my power towards forwarding an arrangement of the business in which you are involved.'

Gower had not got a great reputation in the eyes of many of his contemporaries but the evidence does suggest that he had instructed Shairp to do as much as he could on Bellingham's behalf and he himself had also made the promised representations. There was also the continual financial support that Bellingham had received. However, there was the issue of relationships between England and Russia which were in a deteriorating state. Eventually Gower would have to leave Russia under these conditions and Bellingham would remain in custody.

Bellingham was not content to stay silent and continued to look for any assistance he could to obtain his objects of release and compensation. A letter of 23 September 1808 from the British Mission once again made clear that the British representatives could not get involved because the matter was in the hands of the Russian courts. It confirmed that both the Consul and Vice-Consul had made representations in the matter. Bellingham seemed to be at the end of his routes for redress of his complaints so he made one last attempt to gain his freedom. He arranged for a petition to be placed before the Senate in St Petersburg on 14 December 1808. However,

ALEXANDER I.

Alexander I.

he now made the audacious step of petitioning the Emperor of Russia, Alexander I to support it. The petition in full reads:

'To His Most Imperial Majesty Alexander Pavlovitch, emperor and autocrator of all Russia &c &c &c. Petition of John Bellingham, British subject as follows:

'The petitioner has been detained in the Empire of Russia near five years – the last two years and a half, he has been under criminal & civil arrest in St Petersburg, the former being done away the College of Commerce proceeded to final judgment on the charge on the 3d June last 1808 & in consequence thereof referred to the Liquidation commission to bring the affair to the final arrangement and furnish the necessary clearance that he might obtain his pass for his departure, but not withstanding that reference & his repeated solicitations so to do, the said commission positively refuses to espouse his cause.

'Therefore he most humbly implores your Imperial Majesty will most graciously order said commission to furnish him with the necessary clearance & at the same time remunerate him for the loss of time occasioned to his prejudice by such long detention.

'The petitioner most humbly implores your Imperial Majesty to pronounce a favourable sentence; the present petition written by *Kia Blagotchef* is to be presented to the Senate 1st expedition 14 Dec 1808.'

The petition was translated into Russian and signed on Bellingham's behalf by a notary.

This is a remarkably short petition which is unusual for Bellingham. It revealed the tendency for manipulation by Bellingham and his continual attempts to get money. He stated that the College of Commerce were 'to bring the affair to the final arrangement and furnish the necessary clearance that he might obtain his pass for his departure'. This was not the truth or, in a more modern phrase, he was being economical with the truth. The College had in fact been mandated to get Bellingham to pay the money and if he did not comply to declare him a bankrupt. Only if he paid would there be any pass issued and there was certainly no compensation to be given. However, Bellingham asks the Emperor to also 'remunerate him for the loss of time'. No response came from the Royal Palace and Bellingham would remain in the custody of the Russian authorities.

We have no way of knowing what happened next with Bellingham as there are no official Russian papers to give their side of the story. There is on file one hand-written letter in Russian dated 17 July 1807. A translation of the letter done on 30 March 1808, inserts the wrong date (17 June). It reaffirms that the Senate have examined the case and confirmed a 2000r debt. It also suggests that Bellingham was uncooperative and makes clear he is declared bankrupt and is to be detained. Bellingham left Russia around October and landed in England in early December 1809. There is no independent explanation as to why he was released. In Bellingham's own words:

> 'At length the Senate, quite tired out by these severities, in 1809 I received, at midnight, a discharge from my confinement, with a pass, and an order to quit the Russian dominions, which was in fact an acknowledgment of the justice of my cause.'

Again, as we look at Bellingham's character we see again this blinkered belief that his being allowed to leave Russia 'was in fact an acknowledgement of the justice of my cause'. There is no evidence to support such a claim. What we do know is that the Russian Senate and Courts were adamant on the payment of the claim and all records that are available show that they never wavered in their belief that Bellingham was responsible for the debt. His release therefore was due to circumstances that are not known and certainly what is known does not support Bellingham's claim to justification of his cause. On his arrival in England one would suspect any normal thinking man would hurry home to his wife and discover if the second child had been safely brought into the world. As we shall see this was not the case.

Chapter 7

Statements of grievances

Evidence obtained from Liverpool in 1812 showed that Bellingham did not wait at St Petersburg for a direct ship to England. He obtained passage to Sweden and from Gothenburg, in the company of four businessmen, sailed to London in December 1809. There are more unanswered questions raised about Bellingham's journey. Where did he get the money to pay passage to Sweden and on to London? Did the businessmen he travelled with meet his costs? What is remarkable is that Bellingham had not seen his wife for over two years. She now had two children, a son born in Russia and a son born in Wigan, who he had never seen. What kind of character is it who does not immediately go home to this family but rather stays in London? In fact, his wife was not even aware he has returned. She learned of this from Bellingham's cousin Ann Scarbrow, now Billet, in a letter written from her London home. This was the young girl who had played with Bellingham and with whom he had spent many happy childhood years in St Neots; she was now a reasonably well-off widow. The presumably penniless Bellingham, forever stating that he is never supported, had found himself once more benefitting from the generosity of another. Eventually Bellingham would write to his wife and inform her of his whereabouts.

As he settled into Ann's home that December in 1809, he exposed the fantasy that he now believed as real. His wife came down to London to join him for Christmas 1809 and he informed her and Ann that now he had returned from Russia, he had realised £100,000 (£7.25m) with which he intended to buy an estate in the West of England and a house in London. He admitted that he had not got the money but said it was the same as if he had, for he had gained his cause in Russia and the Government would make good all the loss he had sustained. He repeatedly told them that this was 'assuredly the fact'. The only sure thing about his claim was its nonsense. He had not gained anything in Russia except a long spell in prison and detention, often on bread and water and every legal statement had made clear he owed money and not the reverse. This incredible belief would underpin his delusions and subsequent actions. On considering Bellingham's mental state demonstrated in the incident, we see a classic delusional state, in which the person suffering from it cannot tell what is real from what is imagined. Strong features of this disorder are unshakable beliefs in something untrue or which are not based on reality. In reality, however, the situations are either not true at all or highly exaggerated. In Bellingham's case, he appeared to display persecutory delusion in which he believed that he was being mistreated. It is not uncommon for people with this type of delusional disorder to make repeated complaints to legal authorities.

Later records would show that in pursuit of his delusion he would go to extreme lengths to try and convince his wife and Mrs Billet that he was not mad in his claims because they did not believe him. Mrs Billet said:

> '... but neither she nor I gave any credit to it; he then told Mrs. Bellingham and myself, to convince us of the truth of it, he would take us to the secretary of state's office; he did so, and we saw Mr. Smith the secretary. When Mr. Smith came to us, he told Mr. Bellingham that if he had not known that he had ladies with him, he would not have come at all. Mr. Bellingham then told him the reason he had brought us, that it was to convince us that his claim was just, and that he should very soon have the money. Mr. Bellingham said – "Sir, my friends say that I am out of my senses, is it your opinion, Mr. Smith, that I am so?" Mr. Smith said, "It is a very delicate question for me to answer, I only know you upon this business, and I can assure you, that you will never have what you are pursuing after", or something to that effect. We then took our leave of Mr. Smith, and when we got into the coach, he took hold of his wife's hand, and said, now I hope my dear, you are well convinced all will happen well, and as I wished, and as he had informed us, to which we felt indignant, that he should have taken us to an office, and made us appear in the light he did.'

This clearly demonstrates the mental state of Bellingham. Despite being told in front of his wife and Mrs Billet that he 'will never have what you are pursuing after', he told his wife that he hoped she was 'well convinced all will happen well'. In considering if Bellingham is truly insane in his delusion, the evidence is that he was able to continue conducting complex business arrangements and communicating in a very normal manner. This is another aspect of delusional disorder; people with it often continue to socialize and function normally, apart from the subject of their delusion. The incident also led his wife to contemplate a separation from him. Mary had had enough of his strange behaviour and neglect of her and the children. Ann Billet and her uncle James Neville talked her into staying with Bellingham.

After this, he wrote to Richard, 1st Marquess Wellesley at the Foreign Office. It contained the usual account of Bellingham's claims of injustice and ill treatment in Russia. It enclosed the documents to the Russian government and Bellingham's various letters to the other Russian authorities and the British ambassador in St Petersburg. It contained the insistence that the British Government had to make good the compensation Bellingham believed had been due to him from the

Russian state. As would be expected, Wellesley's secretary Charles Culling Smith wrote on 30 January 1810 to inform Bellingham that the Government could not interfere in the case 'in some measure, by the circumstances of the case itself, and entirely so at the present moment by the suspension of intercourse with the Court of St Petersburg'.

It was apparent with any normal interpretation that the diplomatic language was clearly stating that the case itself had no grounds and that relations with Russia would prevent even any attempt to seek redress there. However, Bellingham would not let the matter go. He was now focussed on only one thing, financial compensation. On 16 February 1810, he made a petition to the Treasury outlining his claims and insistence of an injustice done to him. Had he not, he argued, lost all his mercantile business and reputation? Had he and his family not suffered great loss and were now in financial ruin? He again insisted the government must pay him compensation. Here we see this character trait of Bellingham in his petition. He is totally innocent of all blame and someone else must take responsibility and reimburse him for his losses. There is a pathetic blinkeredness in Bellingham that cannot see outside of his own sense of injustice. For him there is no grey in the matter. It is a black and white case that must, in his opinion, clearly show that he is in the right. It is no surprise that the Secretary to the Lord's Treasury replied:

'Treasury Chambers Feb. 24 1810
'Sir,
    'Having laid before the Lord's Commissioners of his Majesty's Treasury your petition of the 16th instant, submitting a statement of losses sustained by you in Russia, and praying relief, I am commanded by their Lordships to return to you the documents transmitted therewith, and to acquaint you that my Lords are not able to afford you any relief.
'I am &c.
'Geo. Harrison'

Bellingham's records show that throughout this time he was also conducting business as an agent, dealing with cargo from Sweden and Ireland. These documents show that this trade was also not without disputes. The notes confirm that he had income and instead of this income being directed towards his family he was using it to remain in London and pursue what he believed to be his quest for righteousness and justice.

In May he was again writing, once more laying out in detail his claims and arguments for compensation. The response has inevitability about it:

'Council Office, Whitehall, 16 May 1810

'Sir,

'I am directed by the Lords of the Council to acquaint you, that their Lordships having taken into consideration your petition on the subject of your arrest in Russia, do not find that it is a matter in which their Lordships can, in any manner, interfere.

'I am, Sir, &c
'W Fawkner'

Clearly, the realisation of the delusion of his West Country house and a London residence and his assertion to his cousin and wife of its certainty, was so entrenched in Bellingham's mind that he could not give up. His next step was to write to the Prince Regent, somehow believing that such an action would result in success. This pattern follows the Russian progress when he appealed to the Emperor after all doors were closed. This time he began to include the idea of national disgrace. The response was again predictable – nothing could be done by His Royal Highness and he is pointed to the politicians.

Bellingham's reaction was to continue to present an unshaken faith in his right to justice and compensation. He is not in any way deflected from his cause:

'Having then understood that any remuneration which I might conceive myself entitled to, I could only procure through the medium of Parliament, I applied myself to several Members of Parliament, to ascertain what line of conduct I ought to pursue in order to obtain that desirable end.'

It is undoubtedly true that the one thing the deluded should not be given is false hope that their delusion is real. Despite the passage through the Russian legal system and two clear indications from the English state authorities that there can be no hope of any resolution for his cause, Bellingham continued to believe that he could defy all reality. He turned to Members of Parliament for direction. If ever there was an opportunity to try and bring Bellingham to face the truth of his delusional situation and turn away from a destructive path back to his family, it was here. However, the understanding of mental illness was virtually non-existent and the chance was lost. He was further encouraged with fateful advice:

'These gentlemen told me that I should make application to the Chancellor of the Exchequer – thus petitioning for leave to bring in a petition upon a subject which, bring well founded, became a matter of right, and not a favour.'

'A matter of right and not a favour' are words that speak volumes as to Bellingham's mind-set. In his delusion, there was no possibility of his not getting the result he sought. These men have now convinced him that he was due this result as a right and not a favour. The person they directed him to was Spencer Perceval, the Chancellor of the Exchequer and First Minister. He had now become the person responsible to ensure Bellingham would be able to obtain his 'justice' and resulting compensation. It was therefore to him that Bellingham wrote a long missive setting out his arguments and demands for compensation, much the same as in all other communications. He personally took it to Downing Street and handed it over to Michael Herries, Perceval's Private Secretary. However, Bellingham was again thwarted in his ambition, returning to Downing Street on 22 May to be told by Herries, 'Mr Perceval could not give his permission for the introduction of his petition'. This was confirmed in writing:

Rt Hon Spencer Perceval

An early sketch of Spencer Perceval. Artist Unknown.

'Downing Street, 27 May 1810

'Sir,

'I am desired by Mr. Perceval to state to you, in reply to your letter of yesterday, that the time for presenting private petitions has long since passed; and that Mr. Perceval cannot encourage you to expect his sanction in introducing into the house a petition which Mr. Perceval thinks is not of a nature for the consideration of Parliament.

I am &c.
Thomas Brooksbank'

This is an important stage in understanding Bellingham's character and mental state. He has now reached the point of being told by the chief minister of the land that his cause has no future. He has been specifically discouraged in pursuing the parliamentary route. It is clear that, for the government, this matter is at an end, but not for Bellingham. In his mind, the matter shifted to a personal crusade for his own 'justice'. It had now become, because of Perceval's denial, a matter of 'national honour', another aspect of his delusion that he was more important than he actually was. So, despite Perceval's clear statement, he again wrote to the Lord's Counsel of the Treasury, seeking relief from the government, The reply, dated 2 July 1810, was almost identical to the one received in the previous February. They could not grant him any relief. The door was closed. Bellingham returned to Liverpool and what would follow was a dangerous silence in which the fires of anger would smoulder.

To all observers, it did appear that Bellingham had given up his quest for compensation and relief from the Government. He and his wife had had their heated arguments. Bellingham had insisted on his determination to get his compensation and live the dream life with the proceeds. Mary had pointed out his folly in pursuing these things based on her experience so far in Russia and in London. His return to Liverpool must have brought her much comfort; she now had her husband home again and the boys could now enjoy their father. The couple settled into a normal marriage routine and around mid-July Mary became pregnant again. Her later letters show that she really believed she had persuaded Bellingham to settle down and concentrate on making a living. She was also doing her part in building a millinery business with Miss Mary Stevens. She was younger than Mary Bellingham and whilst an able and astute woman, she did not have the experience of the older Mary. The business was registered in the Liverpool Trade Directory as Bellingham and Stevens, of Duke Street. Her name being first reflected the fact that Mary Bellingham was the more intellectually able of the two and the brains of the business. Mary Stevens' skills were in the practical production of the dresses and hats they created. With their skills in millinery and dressmaking their joint enterprise was quite successful. By the time John Bellingham came home it was doing well.

Stevens would later state that Mary Bellingham had for a 'long time' never heard from her husband, until the letter arrived from Ann Billet. She recalled it was not until the summer of 1810 that he joined them at the home in Duke Street. Later Miss Stevens would confirm that as far as she and Mrs Bellingham understood he had 'relinquished' the idea of getting anything from the government. He then began to look after the millinery accounts for the business. His sister Mary died in April 1810 and she was buried at St Pancras but there are no records to show whether or not Bellingham attended the funeral. On 19 November, Bellingham was informed that she had left £450 (£32,000) in her will and, with her mother dead – a handwritten note on the deed shows that his mother died shortly after her daughter – Bellingham was the sole beneficiary.

We know from a notebook for 1811 that Bellingham kept, he began to broker trades. He acted in the movement of coal, iron and wax between Liverpool and Dublin. He also oversaw cargo from Gothenburg. His notes show that whilst he had some income it was not great. They also reveal his recording meticulous details of the shipments and the income he was receiving and spending. There was also the account of a dispute over a consignment of wax, which once again saw Bellingham writing his usual long and adamant account that he was not at fault and would not

The handwritten note confirming Bellingham's mother's death in 1810.

be paying any money to anyone. The book's pages are littered with what appear to be statements recorded for legal purposes. They begin with 'I John Bellingham …', 'Know that I John Bellingham …', 'I John Bellingham make oath …' and 'Know ye that …'; there then would follow exact statements. Who these were for is not clear but they do seem to be intended in case of a dispute arising or may be further evidence of delusional behaviour. It also may well be that Bellingham had learned a lesson and recorded every single detail should he ever find himself in a similar situation to that in Archangel.

This attempt to establish any business, at this time, was made in the most difficult of circumstances. The world of trade was in flux and the outlawing of slavery had seriously impacted the city of Liverpool; the ensuing economic climate brought a depression in Bellingham's activity. Ireland was no longer the great gold mine for shipments of linen and animals. His Irish contact with his wife's father, Neville, was also in jeopardy as he had also gone through bankruptcy and had fled from Northern Ireland to Dublin. Bellingham would travel to Dublin to meet him and try and regenerate some business. The millinery trade was also under strain; money being tight meant that there was nothing extra for clients to spend on the dresses and hats being produced by the two Marys. The pressure on Bellingham to achieve success and financial improvement was immense but success was thwarted by the financial climate. There was only one way, in his mind, that he was going to change the situation and it was not through a struggling merchants' insurance agency business.

Whilst Bellingham on the surface was a man going about his business, we need to appreciate that underneath he was still a man consumed with a delusional passion to get his compensation and, in his mind, his reputation restored. Whether the situations he had been through were of his own making or not, there was a reality at the root of his delusion. He had endured horrendous imprisonment under terrible conditions. There had been that long separation from his family and he had been through court after court to be told he had no case for redress and that he was liable for debts he believed were not due. In England, he again had hopes of settlement but every door was closed and he remained frustrated at every turn and this reinforced his delusion. His wife, cousin and friends had all advised him to quit the fantasy and settle back into normal life and enjoy his family. So in the matter of his claim, he was alone and isolated and a deep depression and anger grew inside him; the smouldering anger now became a raging fire that could not be quenched without his achieving justice that he sincerely held was due to him.

Mary would confirm that '[her husband] transacted business as a merchant but during that time he did not mention anything about his further application to Government'. His outward demeanour must have been a masterclass in disguising what was happening under the surface. Mary further stated that 'she has never perceived anything like derangement' in her husband during the months he spent with her. John Parton, another merchant in Liverpool, conducted business with Bellingham on a daily basis. He was extremely close to him and he also noted nothing strange, other than being told the details of what happened in Russia, the telling of which made Bellingham a little more animated, thus supporting the idea of his delusional disorder.

He was told by Bellingham that there was 'an insurance claim' due as a result of the difficulties he had experienced. Parton was led to believe that the money Bellingham would get would be used to establish a business partnership between them. It was in December 1811 that Bellingham told Mary, Miss Stevens and Parton that he had to go to London to conduct business on a shipment of iron. He left Liverpool for the last time, leaving his wife in ignorance of his true intent. This intent would be of historical significance and bring the greatest grief to his family.

Chapter 8

A Tragic Crusade

Before he left, he celebrated Christmas with the family and Miss Stevens. They enjoyed the joy of such seasonal occasions and Mary Bellingham was very happy; she had her husband and her children gathered around the family table. As she served up the Christmas meal, she believed that the horrors of the past and the distant dismal and cheerless Christmases spent in Russia were now forgotten. Unknown to Mary, Bellingham had composed further documents to take to London to pursue his cause. On 31 December 1811, he bade farewell to his wife and children, assuring them of a speedy return after he had conducted his own business. He also made arrangements to call on merchants in London regarding the supplies of material for the millinery business. As he was waved off from the family home, the intentions in his heart and the papers in his travelling case were completely concealed from all.

On 8 January, Bellingham appeared to be conducting the business of trading in iron. He wrote to Parton in Liverpool, strangely addressing him as 'Dear Sir' instead of the usual 'Parton', informing him of the progress of a deal. The letter was very formal but with no hint of anything other than business. Mary would send a letter to her husband on 18 January and the cheerfulness of the celebrated season was evident. She tenderly wrote to him about Henry, the new born son. He had left the little lad enduring his time of teething and had written to Mary on his arrival in London to enquire after his son's health:

> 'Your letter I received in due course and I am glad to relieve your anxiety regarding darling Henry who is wonderfully recovered and has cut two teeth.'

Mary's belief was that her husband's visit to London would not be long and she reminded him of his mission as she understood it. The millinery business had received a consignment of silk material that was incorrect:

> 'I feel most obliged by your attention in regard to our business, but must request you to call again at Phillips & Davisons as it is their Travellers mistake and not any fault of ours.'

She heavily underlines this passage to emphasise her point. Reading Mary's letter there is a suspicion that she may not totally trust her husband. She seems unsure of her husband's purpose in going to London:

> 'I feel much surprised at your not mentioning any time for your return, you will be three weeks gone on Thursday, and you know I cannot do anything with regard to settling the Business until you return.'

This was a reference to the fact that Bellingham had decided to hand the whole millinery business over to Miss Stevens. He was to finalise the account books and make the legal arrangements for the transfer. In that decision, we have a clue that Bellingham believed there would be no need of the extra income when he came into possession of his 'compensation'.

The fact was that despite his business activities and the money Mary was bringing in, they were still struggling financially. She warned him, 'We have got very little Money since you left' and went on in her letter to remind him of his family responsibilities:

> 'I think I need not instruct you to act with economy, your feeling for your family will induce you to do it.'

This is a telling phrase as to Bellingham's character and his attitude to money. She writes of not needing to instruct him but then does. Her appeal is to his feelings for his family. Why would she need to write this? Mary was an Irish girl from the tough North of Ireland. She had seen her own father constantly make bad business decisions and go bankrupt; by now she had realised that her husband was of a similar cut. He had flown off in flights of fancy about great business deals. He had been seen in Russia to act in the strangest ways and refuse to accept the obvious nature of his situation. There can be no doubt that she knew her husband well, and underneath her apparent acceptance that he was going to act correctly, she had suspicions and needed to remind him of what he should be focussed on – his family. She ended the letter sending him kisses from 'the Children' and from 'Mamma', signing it 'yours very affectionately'. She added a P.S. showing her anxiety about his absence, 'Pray let me know when you will return.' All the kisses and all the affection seemed not to have touched Bellingham; he was set on his own course and would not be deflected.

Bellingham had established himself in lodgings at 9, New Millman Street. His landlady, Mrs Rebecca Robarts – sometimes her name was recorded as Roberts – was delighted to welcome him back. He had stayed with her previously and had been 'the perfect lodger'. Indeed, the good landlady noted that he was 'a pious man and church goer' and described him as a 'distinguished man'. She would say he was of low spirits but quite a stable character. From her house, he would conduct his campaign for redress from government. In spite of Mary's caution about money, he was paying 10s 6p per week plus 5s for using the fire. On top of this would be food and washing costs along with printing expenses he would incur, which in one case was £9 15s 0d (£640). His living expenses alone were around £1 per week (£48). Back in Liverpool that money would have gone much further in the hands of Mary, than in his in London.

However, that was not Bellingham's concern. Three days after Mary had written to him, he began his crusade for his cause. He penned a memorial to the Prince Regent, once more outlining his experiences in Russia and the hardships endured. He set out what he believed was a case for the government to make good his financial losses. This time he claimed the sum of £6,000 (£385,000). This was the figure he had given when writing to Parton in Liverpool, although he would later say he had been told by Bellingham that it was between £8,000 (£513,000) and £10,000 (£641,500) he was asking for. Bellingham also wrote to him on 24 January informing him of his writing to the Prince Regent. In the letter, he makes him aware of his deception with Mary, telling him, 'I write to Mrs B, as you will hear, not exactly as it is, but what I wish her to think, regarding my stay in town.' We see in this the Jekyll and Hyde nature of Bellingham, who demands the truth and honesty from others, whilst he himself is prepared to deceive. In the letter, he notes that he has mislaid the original petition he had written. Later, that loss would be explained by a painful discovery in Liverpool.

His letter to the Prince Regent was answered on 18 February 1812, and he had passed the buck to his Privy Council:

> 'I am directed by Mr Sec. Ryder [The Home Secretary] to acquaint you that you petition to his Royal Highness the Prince Regent, has been referred, by the command of His Royal Highness, for the consideration of his Majesty's Most Honourable Privy Council.'

It is a desperate man who looks for hope wherever he can find it. On 20 February 1812 Bellingham immediately wrote to Parton in Liverpool. It is obvious that he has been lifted to a state of euphoria by the response:

> 'I have the pleasure to inform you that on the day His Royal Highness came into power he immediately put my affair in train as you will perceive from the annexed copy of a notice I received yesterday morning from the Secretary of State's office. The business is now going forward by royal authority and I will very soon receive my damages. [The Regency had actually begun on 5 February 1811]'

It is clear from the records that those in authority were aware of the previous desperate attempts that had been made to get damages. They could have been in no doubt that there was no prospect of any settlement for Bellingham. It is therefore cruel that they should give him any encouragement to hope otherwise. This encouragement now allowed him to inform Parton that he could tell Bellingham's family. However, there would be no need for him to do this.

Mary Bellingham had been at home in Liverpool and was no doubt further concerned about her husband's absence with no idea of his return. She had been looking through his papers in a desk and had discovered documents from Bellingham's solicitor and notes of the mislaid petition to the Prince Regent. This woman, struggling with little money, had trusted her husband's word that he had abandoned the pointless crusade against the government. Her life had been a continual round of standing beside her husband through the most horrendous experiences in Russia. She had supported him in his many fantastic business enterprises and bankruptcy therefrom, had borne him children and took the greatest part of responsibility in caring for them in the frequent absences of their father. Her search through his papers must have been with a desperate feeling of anxiety that she hoped would be relieved in finding that all was in order. The disappointment in discovering that she had been lied to and betrayed could only have been devastating for this faithful wife.

Mary contacted Parton only to have her worst fears confirmed when he made her aware of the letters from her husband. He told her that Bellingham had been 'meditating for some time' on his plans. The rosy glow of Christmas and the family gathering had gone. The hopes and dreams of a settled future for the family lay shattered by her discovery. Her health went into decline both from the worry about her husband and the worsening financial problems she was experiencing. The lack of money would mean her sons could no longer go to school as the fees could not be paid. She needed more support than was available from the younger Miss Stevens. She needed her husband and he had now abandoned her, pursuing his own lost cause. She would later say that he had deserted her 'in a time of greatest need'. Perhaps it is this deception that best of all betrays the truth about John Bellingham and shows him as a disturbed, selfish self-absorbed individual.

On 28 February 1812, Bellingham sought out a solicitor, Thomas Windle, who prepared an elaborate petition for him. Two scrap pieces of paper in Bellingham's records show that, with Windle, he had despaired of help from Lord Gower and wanted to go to Carlton House to meet Colonel John McMahon. He was the Private Secretary to the Prince Regent and Bellingham believed, 'I cannot fail of success if I make an interview with Col. McMahon'. It appears that Colonel McMahon 'mislaid' the original petition and 'another account' had to be drawn up by Bellingham. Windle, in the process of assisting Bellingham and preparing documents, experienced him flying into rages when Lord Gower was discussed (another symptom of the delusion) and noted that he had received apologies

The heading of Bellingham's grand petition to Parliament.

for these outbursts from Bellingham. The grand petition was entitled, 'To the Honourable the House of Commons of the United Kingdom of Great Britain and Ireland in Parliament assembled'. The sub-heading read, 'The Humble Petition of JOHN BELLINGHAM of Liverpool, Merchant'. The original is a grand half by three-quarter metre document in beautiful copperplate script, designed to impress. Indeed, it was first sent to the Prince Regent to have his approval for it to go before the House.

The lengthy document once more set out Bellingham's version of events in Russia. He described in dramatic detail his first detention when he was 'seized and dragged' from his carriage at Archangel. In recounting the claims against him in Russia, he very much painted himself as innocent. There is then set out his views on the actions of Sir Stephen Shairp and Lord Gower. His account noted their acting on his behalf but he makes clear his belief that they were ineffective, as he saw it, and did not do enough. Again, there is the insistence that he was 'ill-used' and 'illegally detained'. He bemoans the six months spent in Archangel and then wrote of his going to St Petersburg. There followed his statements that he had already made in Russia to the Justice Minister, Count Kotzebue, laid out in the very same format. It recounted the claims of an invalid oath, the allegation of a false statement by the Russian Governor and being thrown into prison by him. He restated his claim that the *Procureur* of Archangel had declared that he was correct in his charges against the authorities at Archangel and was given a document to obtain 'Indemnification for his suffering'. This particular document has not been found but other Russian items were found among his possessions.

The story of the legal process is related in the document. He again painted the drama of events:

> 'That although your Petitioner's Case was irrefutable, yet the Senate instead of answering to your Petitioner's Complaints, or redressing his grievances, patronized the proceedings, and in consequence had your Petitioner arrested and imprisoned on various erroneous allegations, the

Russian documents, dated 1809 & 1812, that were found among Bellingham's effects after he was arrested.

erroneousness of which their own Courts were afterwards obliged to furnish official testimony ; after having tortured your Petitioner for a series of years, sometimes by closely confining him in a wretched loathsome Prison, at others condemned to a Dungeon, to be kept on bread and water, often marched publicly through the City with gangs of Felons and Criminals of the worst description, and even then by the house of his Majesty's resident; at best, he was never suffered to go out but like a Person under serious Criminal Arrest, and was the object of attention, not only of all the Foreign Ministers resident at the Court, but of the Public at large, to the great disparagement of his Majesty's Crown, and the heart rending humiliation of himself.

'Through the whole course of these proceedings your Petitioner made innumerable applications to the Consul and Ambassador for an Appeal to the Emperor on such a National Disgrace, and was not only uniformly rejected, but the Consul went so far as to assert the proceedings to be right.'

This again helps with insight to Bellingham's state of mind. He had been treated terribly and of that there was no doubt. However, he never takes any responsibility for his actions that led to that situation. He further repeated the belief that his own humiliation is linked to a 'National Disgrace'. Therefore, in his view, that in turn was a 'disparagement' of the king himself. In this threefold humiliation of Bellingham, the nation and the king, Lord Gower did not do anything to deal with it and in fact agreed with it. This was even more galling to Bellingham because he had been humiliated in front of Lord Gower's very own residence. This was a grave injury to him and would become a key reason for Bellingham's subsequent actions and underpinned his delusion. He further laments:

> 'Thus without having offended any Law, either Civil or Criminal, and without having injured any individual, in this manner was your Petitioner bandied from one Prison to another, through the various ministrations of Lord Granville Gower, Mr Stuart, the Marquis of Douglas, and Lord Leveson Gower's second Embassy, and two years subsequent thereto.'

It is notable that Gower got a second mention and, as we will discover later, Bellingham had a particular grudge against him for what he saw as his dereliction of duty. He reinforced this attitude by quoting from another case in Russia in which Gower was involved:

> 'That during this period a dispute happened betwixt a Captain Gardner of Hull, and the Captain of a Guard Ship, on a squabble of only two roobles for Pilotage, which trifling affair was carried to the Emperor no less than four times by His Majesty's Minister within the space of two months, while your Petitioner's case was sedulously suppressed, although the honour of both countries was materially concerned in the issue.'

The wound in Bellingham was obviously very deep as he continued his tirade against Gower. He had left Russia with Sir Stephen Shairp and his replacement is also criticised for not helping him. Bellingham felt abandoned:

> 'Thus both the Consul and Ambassador left St Petersburg, leaving your Petitioner the Object of Persecution, without any aid whatsoever.'

The use of capitals in 'Object of Persecution' is to emphasise the strength of his feelings and reveals his delusion's foundation. He confirmed the Russian authorities released him in October 1809 and he asserted the release was a revocation of the charges against him.

Bellingham then recounted the arrival back in England and laid out the litany of people who he had called upon to help. This included Richard Wellesley and the Lords of His Majesty's Treasury but they had rejected his requests and were unable to help. He strangely claimed that his case and documents were 'investigated by His Majesty's most Honourable Privy Council, and found to be perfectly correct'. This of course was not the case and betrayed the blinkered way Bellingham looked at his situation. He underscored the tragedy of his case, describing it as 'a long series of Cruelty and Oppression'. Furthermore, his 'Health and Reputation' were 'materially injured' and he had lost his business. Also, his 'whole Property' had been absorbed in supporting 'the Expenses' and making good the 'Consequences of the Proceedings'. – note the use of capitals again. He is a man who is certain of his case. He is convinced that someone is responsible for restoring his reputation and financially compensating him:

> 'Your Petitioner humbly conceives, that having undergone such a series of Persecution, solely on account of his having applied for redress for the injury sustained by the Letter of General Punter, the Governor General of Archangel, to Sir Stephen Shairp, hereinbefore stated, he presumes it renders the Adair of National Import, as such – and that the Consul and Ambassador having neglected and declined interfering in his Behalf with the Emperor, which your Petitioner is of opinion they ought to have done, your Petitioner therefore humbly thinks, that in Justice, he is entitled to Satisfaction for the Damage he has sustained from the Government of this Country therefore, most humbly prays your Honourable House to take into its Consideration your Petitioner's Case, and recompence your Petitioner for the Losses he has actually sustained in consequence of the Circumstances for his Personal Sufferings, as your Honourable House may judge right and proper.'

Having laid out his case and expressed his claims, Bellingham was certain that he would have the Royal assent and settlement from Parliament.

Whilst conducting this run of correspondence to the various people, Bellingham was also continuing to look after his merchant business. On 4 March 1812, he wrote to his business partner Parton and the introduction in the letter was very calm and business-like. He was arranging for a shipment of iron to come from Dublin to Liverpool and the payments were all in order. He then continued the letter and expressed confidence that 'my other concern [his seeking compensation] will be very soon finally arranged to my satisfaction'. There is no doubt he was aware of the problem getting compensation as he recognises where it comes from:

> 'My compensation must come out of the public money for which Parliament alone has the disposal.'

He explained to Parton the process of the next few steps and assured him that 'I am however perfectly satisfied that there will be no unavoidable delay'. He further informed him that he will not 'quit town' until the matter is settled, which he hoped would be '3 to 4 weeks'. He ended by asking for a pair of boots to be sent to him by 'first coach'. There follows a lengthy postscript with further details about the cargo of iron.

No doubt he believed his next visit would be to the Houses of Parliament and he was very keen to appear respectable. To this end, on 5 March he also decided to get repairs done to his clothing. He went to the premises of the aptly named James Taylor and had a pair of pantaloons and a waistcoat made. Taylor would describe the fitting of the waistcoat at Bellingham's lodgings, with Bellingham complaining it was too tight and he had another one made.

His sensitivity to his sartorial elegance was not needed. On 9 March, he got the reply that would bring disappointment:

'Whitehall, 9 March 1812.'

'SIR,

'I am directed by Mr. Secretary Ryder, to acquaint you, that your Petition to His Royal Highness the Prince Regent, praying that he would be pleased to order your Memorial I there'n inclosed, addressed to the House of Commons, to be brought before Parliament has been laid before His Royal Highness, and that he was not pleased to signify any commands thereupon.

Your Memorial to the House of Commons is accordingly herewith returned.

'I am, Sir,

Your most obedient,
Humble Servant,
J. BECKETT.'

We have further insight into Bellingham's character as he reacted to this news. He had approached the highest authority in the land and had been told that there was no case to move the matter forward. However, he was not content with that reply and decided to take upon himself the laying of the petition before every Member of Parliament. His hope was that at least one of them would take up his cause and bring the matter to the House. On 12 March 1812, he composed a letter that informed the MPs of his attempts to get redress and of the final rejection by the Prince Regent. He laid the pathos of his experiences as he saw them on thickly:

'Having borne the weight of this unhappy affair abroad, for a series of years, in a manifold way – on my return home I had the mortification to find my affairs gone to ruin, – my property sold up, – my Family distracted, and suffering in the most severe manner by the inevitable ruinous consequences of my detention, – and for the preceding two years they had not been able to ascertain whether I was alive or dead. Since my return I have not only been bereaved of a further property, (bequeathed in my absence) to make good the consequences of this business, but am now considerably involved – so fatal has it proved. – Thus circumstanced, I trust I shall be pardoned in addressing the House of Commons individually, in the hope that on the behalf of material justice some Member will do me the favour to bring forward my said just Petition. – As common justice is all I solicit, and what everyone will agree I ought to have, more especially as my sufferings far the last eight years have been almost too great for human nature to sustain.'

There is no doubt that he had suffered but as before he appears to be in denial of his own behaviour that contributed to his prolonged detention. He was still resolutely convinced that he should have 'justice' and financial compensation for his Russian experience.

It is apparent that General Isaac Gascoyne, the member for Liverpool, was particularly pressed by Bellingham to bring the matter forward as Bellingham's local representative. About 13 March 1812, he met Bellingham at his home in Mayfair. He gave a little hope to Bellingham but stressed it was on condition that there was evidence to support all the claims Bellingham was making. Furthermore, he informed him that an approach would have to 'memorialise His Majesty's Ministers'. As a result of this meeting, on 17 March 1812, Bellingham wrote once more to Richard Ryder, the Home Secretary seeking permission to present the Petition to Parliament:

'Having had the honour to speak with several members of the House of Commons on the subject of my intended petition to Parliament, all processioned applications must come from the side of His Majesty's Ministers. I am therefore instructed by them to apply for permission to bring forward my said petition as an absolute necessary preliminary measure.

Most humbly soliciting the liberty to do so
I have the honour to be
Sir, your humble and very obedient servant,
John Bellingham
London 17 March 1812'

He uses an interesting phrase: 'instructed to do so'. He has taken the advice not as guidance but as an instruction. In this there is an impression with Bellingham that this course of action will produce the results he wants – because MPs have instructed him. Ryder therefore must obey that instruction. As a result, on

18 March 1812 he also wrote to Parton informing him that he hoped to be back in Liverpool within the week, 'as the good affair will be in a measure decided'. His optimism was short lived. The reply from Ryder was not favourable and would have tragic consequences:

> 'Whitehall, 20 March 1812.
>
> 'Sir,
>
> 'I am directed by Mr. Secretary Ryder to acknowledge the receipt of your letter of the 17th instant, requesting permission, on the part of his majesty's ministers, to present your petition to the House of Commons; and in reply I am to acquaint you, that you should address your application to the right Hon. the Chancellor of the Exchequer.
>
> I am, &c.
> J. Beckett'

Ryder had placed the Chancellor of the Exchequer Spencer Perceval, who was also Prime Minister, and who had already rejected the petition, firmly into the firing line.

Two years earlier, Bellingham had been told by Perceval that he had no intention of allowing a petition to be presented and Bellingham realised he had come full circle. Every avenue had been closed to him and it would seem that sense would dictate that he should return home to his family. In his mind, though, there was no possibility that he would abandon his course for what he believed was justice. On 23 March 1812, he once more took up his pen. This time he wrote to the police magistrates. Here in the criminal court he expected to put Perceval and his government under their jurisdiction and have them brought to account. This letter revealed the workings of Bellingham's mind and the direction he was now considering going:

> 'To their Worships,
> the Police Magistrates
> of the Public Office in Bow-street.
>
> Sirs, – I much regret its being my lot to have to apply to your worships under most peculiar and novel circumstances.—For the particulars of the case, I refer to the enclosed letter of Mr. Secretary Ryder, the notification from Mr. Perceval, and my petition to parliament, together with the printed papers herewith. The affair requires no further remark, than that I consider his majesty's government to have completely endeavoured to close the door of justice, in declining to have, or even to permit, my grievances to be brought before parliament, for redress, which privilege is the birth right of every individual. The purport of the present is, therefore, once more, to solicit his Majesty's Ministers, through your medium, to let what

is right and proper be done in my instance, which is all I require. Should this reasonable request be finally denied, I shall then feel justified in executing justice myself—in which case I shall be ready to argue the merits of so reluctant a measure with his Majesty's attorney-general, wherever and whenever I may be called upon so to do. In the hopes of averting so abhorrent, but compulsive an alternative, I have the honour to be,

Sirs, your very humble and obedient servant,

John Bellingham.'

In what appears to be a calm considered preamble, he laid out his grievances and, now that as all doors have been closed, it is the magistrates' duty to see that justice is done. They, Bellingham argued, should bring him and the attorney-general together so that he can present his case. Later, John Read, the chief magistrate at Bow Street, stated that he had been in his office and a clerk brought in a package, which contained the letter and 'some papers'. He claimed he did not examine the papers but read the letter and decided that it was something the magistrates could 'not interfere in'. He repackaged the papers and told his clerk to 'to deliver them to the person that brought them when he called again' with a note of his decision. That decision was to inform the Treasury of Bellingham's visit and the general contents of the letter.

In trying to understand Bellingham it is important to note that despite the desperate letters and emotions that were surrounding them, he continued to conduct normal business. On 25 March 1812, he received a letter from a J. Miller in Dublin regarding the cargo of iron he was handling. On the 28th (Easter Saturday), he wrote a brief note to Parton about the deal and discussed the contract he was negotiating. He ended the letter with reference to his latest attempts to get compensation. There is no doubt Bellingham was reaching a crisis point and that there was desperation within him. There is even the thought that 'the old gentleman' (the ailing George III) would even be brought into it 'if it were possible'. He wrote that the matter was once more going to the Treasury and he expected the 'arduous journey' to be ending shortly. 'Everything else,' he wrote, 'will find its level.'

On 1 April 1812, Bellingham arrived at Bow Street again and was given the papers and covering note. He opened them in the presence of the clerk, who said Bellingham removed the petition to the House of Commons and they had a conversation. The full conversation is not known but the clerk apparently directed him to the Treasury once more. The final line of Bellingham's letter was chilling, 'in the hopes of averting so abhorrent, but compulsive an alternative' and yet it seemed not to have been detected by the experienced John Read. In the climate of the day with so many angry voices and apparent empty threats, Bellingham was just one more malcontent. Bellingham once more spoke with General Gascoyne who again directed him to Ministers.

On the same day, he began another letter to Parton informing him of more detail of the Dublin correspondence. He discussed the terms of the deal and enclosed a copy of Miller's letter. On a footnote to that copy, he scribbled a note about his crusade for justice. He did not send the letter off immediately and informed Parton that due to the holidays, the Treasury Board would not meet for some days. He told Parton that 'the thing is in so fair a way to a conclusion'. He added a further note at 12 o'clock asking Parton to contact his wife and tell her he cannot respond to a letter he had received from her dated the 29th, 'before the coming week'. He then added a note which is not completely clear in its meaning, not having Mary's letter:

> 'And it would not have been possible for a man wither to say or do more than I have done. My own mind regarding the conduct I have pursued is perfectly [easy?] and I could wish theirs to be the same. When black is white her – ifs – will be [from?], her, best. Till then they are inadmissible.'

From later letters, we know that Mary had raised doubts that he would achieve anything, often using 'if'. He is making it clear that there will be a definite and positive outcome to his pursuit and any 'ifs' are not being entertained by him – he will not admit them into his thinking.

Bellingham continued both his trade and now increasingly his actions to get the 'justice' to which he felt entitled. On 13 April 1812, he once more sat down and wrote to the Treasury; this time, he was writing more out of a desire to show that he had taken every step he could have been reasonably asked to take. On 14 April, he wrote to Parton again. This time he discussed the arrival of a 'bank post' to Parton and on the back of that payment he enclosed a bill. The letter suggests that Bellingham was in need of finance and he wrote that he had been to the Treasury that morning (to deliver his letter) and expressed his belief that his case was 'on the verge of settlement'. Furthermore, he wrote:

> 'I have been at the Treasury this morning to see after my concern, which has not yet been taken into consideration, but very soon will be so – when everything I hope will go forward to our mutual satisfaction but till then it's not possible for me to act in any decisive manner, and the unsettled way my family is in makes me truly miserable'

It is clear that Bellingham's state of mind is in conflict. He wants to be decisive in his action but he still holds a hope that the matter will be settled as he wants. In the meantime, his concern for his family made him truly miserable. These conflicts within him were brewing towards disaster.

Whilst he waited for what he, despite his hope otherwise, knew was an inevitable refusal, he received a letter from his wife on 15 April. The next day he sent his reply to Mary. The usual precise Bellingham made a mistake when replying; instead of writing a letter to his wife as her husband responding on marital and familial matters, he decided to include a long passage addressed to Miss Stevens on the millinery business. Not only this, he also opened both sections with the same address, 'My Dear …'. He appeared to make no distinction between the two women. This tells us that he was entering a more frantic stage where his concentration was not on home and family. There is a brief reference to his son Henry, who he seemed to hold in most affection, but there is no intimate or affection expressed to Mary:

> 'My dear Mary, Yours dated the 12th did not reach my hands till yesterday evening – you have acted right in following my instructions, and the rest leave to my solicitude, as can assure you it is not forgotten. I could have wished you had mentioned where and with whom Henry is and to let me know how the dear Boy goes on. Herewith a few lines for Miss S- for her government in the Business – and which you may consider as the remainder of your letter.'

There is no address to Mary or ending. He just continued to write to Miss Stevens:

> 'My dear Miss Stevens: As my affairs in London are terminating according to wish, you may easily imagine it's my desire for Mrs B- to quit the Business as soon as possible, and for you to come into full possession of it. The money that has been put in I do not look to, my family having had the benefit of a maintenance and the outstanding debts I am willing to take upon me. Therefore, when you come to Town, I will accompany you to the respective Trades people for the arrangements so that I do not see any occasion for irksomeness on your part in seeing these folks. Bring the Books and confide in me to do what is right and proper. You will not be deceived. No part of Mr Carr's money has been paid to me. I have no doubt but you will be able to get and will go with you to Mr Leigh or even Mrs C- in case of need. I hope to be informed when you mean to be here that I may attend you at the Coach: and command my services in every respect wherein I can be in any way useful to you.'

Again, he ended with no address or greeting just a short scribble signature and not the normal full 'John' or 'John Bellingham'. The letter has many errors that are crossed out and amended. This is unusual compared to his other letters and may reveal a deterioration in his mental and emotional state. He is clearing up the business and, in one way or another, believed that there would be money to sort out any debts or expenses relating to the millinery business. Does he suspect that Miss Stevens may not be confident because of his past behaviour? Is that why he reassures her that 'she will not be deceived'?

On 18 April 1812, he received what he described as 'a final and direct answer' from the Treasury:

'Whitehall, 18 April 1812.
'Sir,—I am directed by Mr. Secretary Ryder to acknowledge the receipt of your letter of the 13th instant, requesting to be informed in what stage your claim on his majesty's government for criminal detention in Russia now is. In reply, 1 am to refer you to my several letters of the 18th of February, 9th and 20th of March, by which you have been already informed that your first petition to his royal highness the Prince Regent, praying for remuneration, had been referred to the consideration of the Lords of the Council. That upon your second memorial, praying his Royal Highness to give orders that the subject should be brought before parliament, his royal highness had not been pleased to signify any commands. And, lastly, "in answer to your application to Mr. Ryder, requesting permission on the part of his majesty's ministers to present your petition to the house of commons, you were informed that your application should he addressed to the Right Hon. the Chancellor of the Exchequer.

I am, &c.
J. Beckett.'

There is a feeling of frustration from Beckett and his direction once more pointed Bellingham to Spencer Perceval. Bellingham was now a man who had decided to bring the matter to a conclusion – one way or another.

His next visit was to the offices of the Secretary of State at the Treasury. There he met an official, Mr Hill. Bellingham explained to him his attempts to obtain a solution for his cause. He was told that there was no possibility of anything being done. He was seen as just another person who wanted something from government that could not be given. In asking what else he could do, he was told by Hill that 'it would be useless to apply to government any more' and furthermore, that he was at liberty to do whatever he thought was proper. For Bellingham this was, as he himself said, 'carte blanche to act in whatever manner I thought proper' and now he set his mind determined to bring about his own justice.

On 20 April 1812, he received a response from his wife to his letter of 15 April. Mary was an angry lady:

'Dear John
'If I could think that the prospects held out in your letter I received yesterday even to be realised, I would be the happiest creature existing, but I have been so often disappointed that I am hard of belief. With regard to Miss Stevens going to London ... before she takes the journey do be certain you can make good your intentions, for should you not ultimately be enabled to fulfill them we would be sunk in ruin from not having sufficient means

to meet the tradespeople. We had concluded to work for a few [patrons] but if you really think Mrs C- <u>will settle her bill</u> it will certainly be better for Miss Stevens ... I have not shown Miss Stevens your letter, for should you succeed, I mean with your permission to give up my share in the business to dear Eliza, who is in a distressed situation in New York, as her mother did not leave her a farthing, and she will be obliged to return to her family here. How truly delighted I shall be at having any means of returning her kindness to me and James. ... I cannot help remarking that in writing to Miss Stevens you address her in the same manner as me. Oh it is my dear Miss Stevens & yours truly John Bellingham. Now I cannot help feeling hurt that there is no distinction made between an indifferent person and an affectionate wife who has suffered so much for you and your children – it appears as if I was no more to you than any woman that you were obliged to write a letter so, I confess to a delicate & feeling mind: these are <u>insults,</u> more particularly as my indisposition seems to have been forgotten but if you fell for be anything the change in my appearance will convince you that I have been very ill, as I am now as thin <u>as I ever was</u> – ... If I was to follow your example, six lines might fill my letter – but perhaps I am not worthy of more. I shall expect your answer by return of Post say Thursday: by that time I hope something will be concluded about your affair.

yours truly,
Mary Bellingham'

This is a letter written with passion and hurt. It is 'Dear John' no sense of the 'My Dear ...'. It helps us consider Bellingham's character through Mary's eyes. He has so 'often disappointed' her that she no longer can believe his wild claims. She was a strong woman with children who was working hard to make a living. Of course, she would have loved to come into money but she knew in her heart it would never come through her husband's campaign in London. To this extent she pleaded with him to 'make good' his 'intentions' before Miss Stevens invests much needed resources into her visit to him. She underlined this to express her concerns. The lack of money is also seen as she underlines the need for a bill to be paid. In her pain at her husband's treatment, she still shows her compassion for a friend Eliza who had been good to her. She would wish to give her share of the business to her and not Miss Stevens but she needed her husband's permission. Therefore, she did not show the letter to Stevens until the matter is settled.

The letter then turned to her hurt feelings as a result of his letter. She accused him of writing to Miss Stevens with tenderness but in her emotional state does wrongly state he had written 'yours truly'. However, she felt that his letter made her feel just like any other woman who he was obliged to write to. Here she also released much of the emotion she must have experienced in Russia. She had suffered both for him and the children and he seemed not to have realised that. His attitude in the letter had bitten deeply, to the point that she felt it was an insult – underlining again for effect. In his own blinkered crusade, he had forgotten her. She had now become ill because of his neglect. It appears that on her return to England from Russia her health had improved but now, and she underlined it, she was 'as thin as I ever was'. She is completely in the depths of pain that he had only written six lines in his letter, 'perhaps' she wrote, 'I am not worthy of more'. Her ending is sharp making clear her expectation that he will bring to an end his absence and she wanted to have that confirmed immediately, by return of post. The signature also reveals that there is still an affection in the pain for Bellingham as she ends 'yours truly' - however it is not 'Mary', but 'Mary Bellingham' as the signature. The letter suggests that the strains on the marriage that were evident in early 1810 had once more grown. It demonstrates also that Bellingham was now consumed with his crusade and everything else is becoming secondary. There is no doubt that both Mary and Miss Stevens believed that Bellingham's pursuit of a settlement was in vain and unlikely to succeed. However, there was no suggestion in any of the letters to hand that they ever had an idea of just how far he was willing to take the matter.

We know that on 21 April 1812, Bellingham made his decision to bring an end to his crusade for justice and have his day in court. It was however, not going to be through an orthodox route. He left his lodgings in New Millman Street and took the fifteen-minute walk to Skinner Street. It is worth considering that walk to try and understand the events that would follow. The weather was colder than usual and no doubt Bellingham would have walked briskly. As he walked he would be turning over in his mind his journey that was driving him forward to Skinner Street. He had just read Mary's letter and its stinging rebuke. She and his children had suffered. In his mind, he would be contemplating those days in Russia with its cold climate and the humiliation of his incarceration in dank cells, eating hard bread and drinking filthy water. The many letters and petitions he had filed in Russia were all in vain. He felt he had been abandoned by the British representatives in St Petersburg. As he considered his constant search for help in England from government and every door being closed in his face, his resolve grew harder. His wife's suffering, his children's suffering and his own being 'ill-used' and his wife now too, angry with him, reached a crescendo that came to only one conclusion in his tortured mind – someone must answer and pay for all this.

There was no room in his thinking for any blame on his part to be considered. His cause was just and righteous and the events that would follow would be seen as justified and no court in the land would think otherwise. He stopped at the end of his journey and stood under the sign, 'William Andrew Beckwith – Gunsmith'. He entered the shop and purchased two steel pistols, bullets, gunpowder and a key to screw the pistol together; they were designed as weapons for concealment. Beckwith told him he would have to practise with the pistols as they were very inaccurate over a few feet. He would also later confirm the purchase, charging him four guineas (£300) and giving him 'free advice'. It is important to note here that the type of pistol chosen gives indications of Bellingham's state of mind. These pistols would have to be carefully assembled before use since they were designed for concealment. Before they were to be used, they would require patient preparation; their use would not be in a flood of passion or temper but rather deliberately and thought out. It points entirely to a mind that is set on a single intention and purpose. In his use of the money for their purchase, there is no regard by Bellingham to the poverty expressed by Mary – everything is sacrificed to his one and only object – justice as he saw it.

The pistols were placed in a cloth bag and taken back to his lodgings then they were placed in his room and hidden from the other members of the household. He had taken Beckwith's advice and spent the next few days up in the woods on Primrose Hill. This was a popular venue for Londoners, which had become free from leaseholders in 1811. It was an area favoured for duels and frequented by those who would practise firing their pistols. So it was that Bellingham went to this wooded area and experimented shooting at trees. His conclusion was that if he intended to use the pistols as he planned he would have to fire at point blank range at his target. He therefore decided on a method to conceal the weapons. James Taylor, the tailor, would later recall:

> 'On the 25th of April, I met him in Guildford-street, he informed me that he had a small job to do, and if I would step back with him he would give it me immediately. When I got to the house he asked me into the parlour, he then went upstairs and brought me a dark coloured coat, he gave me directions to make him an inside pocket on the left side, so as he could get at it conveniently, he wished to have it a particular depth, he accordingly gave me a bit of paper about the length of nine inches. He was very particular to have it home that evening.'

These are not the actions of impulse or temper. They are considered, thought through, determined. Think of the character of the man: he has considered what he is going to do; he practised preparing the weapon and realised that putting it together was awkward; he considered his options and concluded that it must be already constructed and concealed, before he used it; he thought about how quickly he could retrieve it from its hidden location. Under his waistcoat in the band of his trousers under a heavy outer coat was too complicated. His large overcoat was the answer but where? There was no pocket big enough. The answer was to sit down and measure the size of the pistol and create a template for a new pocket. There is a cold detachment in this process. Behind it, is the plan to kill. For Bellingham, it is a simple necessary step along the way to achieve his goal. The killing of a human being was secondary to that. The tailor brought the coat with its new pocket back to Bellingham the same evening. Whilst waiting for the return of the coat, he sat down and wrote to Parton in Liverpool:

'Dear Parton

'Not having had the pleasure to hear from you of late, am uncertain wither Hodges is likely to get a vessel through now or not, but hope so, as he may prove a valuable correspondent.

'Notwithstanding, my frustrations are undeniable yet I had a far greater struggle with Government than I expected – the affair is without precedent and has gone to great length – in fact they refused to do anything after having drawn the affair from one to another as long as they could – I have given notice to the Sec. of State in writing that it was not favor I was soliciting but justice according to law and if his ministers continued to refuse such justice I would execute it myself and then by the merits of the case with them in a criminal Court and I am not the man that will submit to the treatment I have experienced without redress – in consequence Mr Ryder reviewed the business and has sent it to the Treasury to adjudge, indeed its very awkward affair for the Gov[ernment] as well as me – the grand difficulty is the circumstances being so peculiar it cannot be settled regularly without Parliament and to Parliament they have an aversion to bring it – a few more days must now absolutely produce something to relieve a heart completely sick by procrastination and its consequences evil to my conscience and family. One consolation is I must speedily and finally triumph be which way it will in opposition to everything but no remuneration I shall ever obtain can begin to be equivalent to what I have been so committedly called upon to suffer for the last years.

'I trust things will soon open in every respect as it is high time for a change and am Dear Parton

yours truly
John Bellingham'

The initial lines of a business nature are not the intention of the letter. This is a man who had decided on a course of action and is compelled to tell someone. He had seen his plea to government being shuttled between one place and another. In his frustration, he had made it clear that he was not seeking anyone to do him a favour; rather in his mind, all he wanted was justice – and he was not getting it. Therefore, there was that chilling and stark warning that was being missed; he would 'execute it' himself. He knew that his intended action would lead to his appearing in a criminal court but he accepted that as his way to get his redress. There was a steely resolution in him. He was not 'the man that will submit' to the treatment the civil service and politicians were giving him, he was a man who had been harshly treated in Russia and now it was a disgrace that here in his own country he was being humiliated. In his mind, parliament had now focussed down to the person of Spencer Perceval. He was the man who had 'an aversion' to bring the matter to the House. Bellingham's confession was of a heart 'completely sick'. He had reached the end of the road and saw evil in the procrastination of government, not only to himself but to his family. No money could ever pay for the suffering he had endured. It was time for a change in his approach – murder was the decision he took.

Oblivious to Bellingham's state of mind, and unknown to him, George Harrison, on behalf of the Treasury Board, wrote a letter to Lord Castlereagh's secretary. It would appear that they were becoming exasperated with the constant bombardment of letters. Harrison's diary noted:

> 'Read two letters from Mr John Bellingham dated 26th Ult & 9th Ins' together with his Petition claiming redress from H M's Government on Account of the Losses & Sufferings experienced by him in consequence of some Criminal Proceedings instituted against him & arising out of Mercantile Transactions in Russia in 1804 and subsequent Years. Transmit the Papers to Mr Cooke & desire he will submit the same to the Consideration of Lord Castlereagh & move his Lordship to favor this Board with his Opinion whether the circumstances of this case are such as would warrant the Interpretation of H M's Government in the manner suggested by the Memorialist or in any other mode.'

The letter he wrote, dated 28 April, passed the buck to Castlereagh and placed on him, as Foreign Secretary dealing with Russia, the responsibility for a decision. The slow wheels of government meant that no one was telling Bellingham what was happening at this time.

On 29 April, Bellingham wrote to Parton a very short note informing him of a shipment of iron from Gothenburg becoming available and that new regulations were coming into force for custom clearance. It is sharp and business like and the signature is 'yours sincerely' rather than the usual 'yours truly'. There is no reference to the pursuit of his claims against the government. That in itself is telling; every other letter to him had given an update of the situation. It seems now that Bellingham had made his own decision and the die was cast. There was no further need to say anything.

Chapter 9

The Normality of Madness

May was colder than usual; indeed, the weather in Britain for the whole year had been abnormal, the coldest since 1799. Mary Sarto, a washerwoman, made her living doing the washing of those who did not want to, or did not have the facilities to clean their own clothes. She lived at no. 10 Woburn Mews off Little Guilford Street, just at the top of New Millman Street. For most able bodied, it was just a five-minute walk to Bellingham's lodgings. On 4 May 1812, she had washed and ironed his clothes and neatly packed them into a basket. She knew Bellingham was one for seeing everything in good and neat order. She entered the house and carried the linen up to his room. She found him writing and was commanded to sit down whilst he continued to write. She watched him, agitated and scribbling; at one point, he screwed up the paper he had been writing on and tossed it into the fire. Eventually he turned to her and gave her 'one dollar' ('dollar' was a word used for an English coin called a crown and is now worth about £16). He asked her for 4d back but she refused and an argument developed about her charging too much for his dressing gown. She insisted she would not give him any change and so she was told to keep it, but he complained about his frills. Mary Sarto noted later she thought him deranged and laughed at him. Catharine Fidgen, a maid at the house, also described him as deranged. She would make an error in her later testimony. She placed this incident as happening on 11 May, but in Bellingham's notebook, the transaction is dated 4 May and has the amounts; it also showed he expected to pay less. This was the last entry in the book.

Afterwards, he made his way to the House of Commons. He took a seat in the gallery to watch the proceedings as he had begun to do on occasion. Another visitor to the galleries in the house would recall seeing him there, Vincent George Dowling, employed as a reporter for a newspaper called *The Day*. His job meant that he spent a lot of time around the Palace of Westminster. He sat in the galleries using opera glasses to view proceedings below in the chamber. He noted Bellingham who also had such a pair and the two of them engaged in conversation with Bellingham wanting Dowling to point out who was who. He identified the members of the Cabinet and particularly pointed out Richard Ryder to him. What was not known until very much later was that Dowling was a paid secret informer for the Home Office. In the dangerous atmosphere of the day, he was to spy on anyone who could

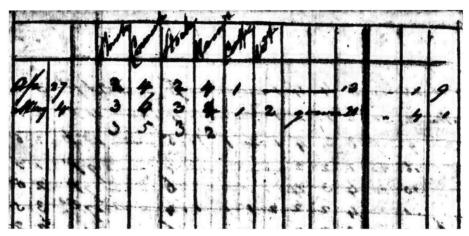

Bellingham's Wash-book showing his detailed entry for May 4 1812 noting the 'gown' the subject of dispute.

be suspected of any plot against the State. There is no doubt that Bellingham's interest would have been noticed by him and his regular reports would have included the meeting. However, no one at the Home Office appears to have taken any notice as in those days there was no systematic procedure for handling the vast amount of paperwork that civil servants received.

On 5 May 1812, a letter simply dated 'May 1812' was sent to Bellingham. It is not signed and ends, 'your most obedient humble servant'. It once more states 'that their Lordships have 'taken into their consideration your several petitions' regarding his 'claims' to suffering in Russia and had referred them to 'His Majesty's Secretary of State for Foreign Affairs [Lord Castlereagh]' who had decided that the matter could not be taken up by the government, 'even if this country were in amity with Russia'. The obedient humble servant had closed the door in Bellingham's face. That afternoon, Miss Mary Stevens had bade goodbye to Mary Bellingham in Liverpool and headed for London. Mary was anxious to see some resolution to the absence of her husband and hoped Miss Stevens might be the instrument to bring about his return to the family. The following day, Mary Stevens arrived in London and settled into her lodgings with Mrs Barker in Kirby Street, less than a mile from Bellingham's in New Millman Street. On Thursday 7 May, she walked there and enquired for Bellingham to be told he was absent from the house. She wrote a brief note which asked him to call on her at Kirby Street the next day; he went to see her as she had requested. From later statements, we can reconstruct the conversation that will help us as we continue to examine his character.

When she first saw him, she noted he had changed in appearance for the worse since she had last seen him at Liverpool. He exchanged greetings with a gentlemanly bow and Miss Stevens immediately shared the concerns she had been charged with by his wife:

> 'Sir, your wife and I have been very hurt to discover that your object of coming to London was not for purposes of business, but to continue to seek application for redress from the Government. Do you not realise how you are losing your time. Your children have also sustained a great loss to their education because of your absence'

There was a violent tone in his response:

> 'You know Miss Stevens it has always been a matter of dissention between me and Mrs B and we should never be happy until it is settled. I am determined to have justice done to me. Indeed I would be undeserving of the name 'parent' if I did not endeavour to make provision for my wife and children. Let us not talk any further on this'

He brought himself back to a calmer state:

> 'I will look at the books for the millinery business tomorrow as agreed. I am going to the Annual Exhibition of the Society of Painters in Watercolours at Spring Gardens tomorrow. Would you and your friend Mrs Barker care to accompany me?'

Bellingham was his usual polite self again and Miss Stevens, sensitive to the difficulty of the situation, agreed.

The morning of Saturday 9 May 1812 once more brought Bellingham to Kirby Street. He was greeted by Miss Stevens in her morning dress and she handed him the books to peruse whilst he sat in the drawing room. She went upstairs and dressed to go out to the exhibition. On her return to Bellingham, she found him going through the books. She decided to raise the issue of his application to Government:

> 'I suppose nothing further has transpired?'
> 'Nothing!' he snapped, 'I have been rather dilatory this week in consequences of your arrival in London.' [he lied] 'However, I shall vigorously set about it on Monday. Now let us go and enjoy the Exhibition.'

As he wandered through the Spring Gardens exhibition looking at the many sketches and watercolours, did he reflect on his own father whose work had also appeared in similar exhibitions? Did he consider that what was about to happen may be associated with his father's madness? He was such a short time away from the momentous event that would not only affect his family but would influence history, yet to all observations he was having a relaxing day in the company of Miss Stevens and her hostess Mrs Barker. As they left the exhibition, Bellingham took them to call at other places, probably in connection with Miss Stevens' trade. They arrived back at Kirby Street and Bellingham collected the books to take away for further examination. He was informed that Miss Stevens was out of town on the Sunday and they agreed he would meet her on Monday morning at 11 o'clock.

Sunday 10 May dawned and, as was his practice, Bellingham went to attend the service at the Chapel of the Foundling Hospital in Guilford Street in the company of his landlady, Mrs Robarts, and her son. He spent the day at his lodgings and had supper alone in the evening. Following supper, the rain was falling heavily and he walked alone to the Magdalen chapel. Mrs Robarts would have normally joined him but she decided against doing so because of the rain. Catharine Fidgen would get the details wrong in later testimony, stating that he and Mrs Robarts went to the Foundling Chapel in the evening. Mrs Robarts' statement to the police contradicted her:

> 'She went with him to the Foundling Chapel on last Sunday morning and she understood he went to the Magdalen in the evening – she was prevented by the rain from going with him'

How does 'a pious man and church goer', who is contemplating murder, sit in two religious services and deal with the dichotomy in his mind of the commandment 'Thou shalt not commit murder' and his belief that what was ahead was justified? Indeed, in a book written at the time, J Hatchard noted the feelings of many:

> 'And what is the most lamentable in this case is that such perversion of morality has not originated in the soul of one of atheistical principles, but of one who professed himself a Christian and went twice to the Church on the Sabbath previous to cool assassination.'

This is something that will be explored later. For now, we know that he had weighed the murder of a man against the suffering he had experienced and believed that at 'the bar of God' he would be acquitted. He was therefore now so purposed. He had no madness in his own eyes but a sincere belief that his decision to execute his justice was a normal response to how he had been treated. This conviction drove him forward to assassination.

Chapter 10

The Assassin's Justice

O n Monday 11 May, in the morning after breakfast, Mrs Robarts suggested to Bellingham that he, along with her and her son would go to the European Museum on Kings Street, St James. This was agreed but first he had to go to see Miss Stevens. Around 11 o'clock, he arrived at her lodgings and returned the books he had been examining. He had written a letter to his wife and one for Parton in Liverpool which he handed in a package to her but she was not finished with him yet; she again wished to talk about his application to the Government:

'When do you expect Parliament to break up? '
'It should be in about two weeks.'
'Would it not be the case that if there is a new Ministry that would retard your concerns? Indeed would it not be better to relinquish it than try to oppose the powerful?'

He looked tired and agitated and snapped:

'I will not! If Ministers refuse to do me justice I will do it myself'
He laid his hand upon his heart, *'you do not know Miss Stevens what I have endured these last six months. I would rather commit suicide than undergo it again'.*
'God forbid that you should commit such an act but your countenance shews what you must have suffered!'

She again noted how much he had changed since he left Liverpool and his family:

'But how are you going to obtain this?'
'I will bring it into a Criminal Court'.
'What do you mean? Is that the Court of the King's Bench?'
'Judgment was given in my favour in the Council and I will compel the Minister to do me Justice as he is the only one who opposed me'.
'I hope all this will finish soon and you might return to your family'.
'I will do all that is in my power to settle it as no person was more inclined to be domestically happy than I. I have given you the letter for Mrs B about the particulars of the millinery business. I wish you good morning and I trust you will have a pleasant journey home.'

With this he left her to return to his own lodgings. The encounter with Miss Stevens had upset him. Despite the dark thoughts that he had shared with her, she remained ignorant of his plans, though the letter she held in her hands to Parton would have enlightened her. The *Lancaster Gazette* printed the shocking portion:

> 'I wish my affairs were come to a conclusion; everything in point of law is in my favour; but Mr Perceval and the ministry have shewn themselves more inclined to favour Lord Gower than do justice to me; however as I am resolved on having justice, in case of need, I will very shortly play a court card to compel them to finish the game.
>
> I am yours sincerely John Bellingham.'

She stated clearly that although violent when talking of his application to government, she detected no signs of madness or intentions to carry out anything more than continue his pursuit for redress.

When he arrived back at New Millman Street, Mrs Robarts noticed he was 'heated and agitated' but he calmed down after a short while. They then set off for the Exhibition and Bellingham suggested he should pay for the boy. She declined and he satisfied himself by buying a book about the exhibition costing one shilling. He went round the exhibition using the book to point out details of the various paintings and artworks on display, to her and her son. After they had finished with the exhibition, they left the hall and headed away from the river to walk along Piccadilly. Bellingham had been holding the boy's hand and he and Mrs Robarts were lost in conversation, when they realised the boy was no longer with Bellingham. He immediately ran back and discovered the boy, and brought him back to his mother. They walked further towards Leicester Square and when they reached Sydney's Alley, he left them. Sydney's Alley contained numerous shops and on his return to them he told Mrs Robarts that he needed to buy a prayer book. He informed her that he had business to see to and he parted company with them. Mrs Robarts would be vital in later days when the matter of Bellingham's sanity would be questioned. She knew him well, not only as a landlady, but as someone who had often accompanied him to church and other outings. She had never observed him as any other than as a sane and normal man. She headed for home and he made his way towards parliament. He had to be there at 4.30 but the diversions with the boy and going to a shop had delayed him. He now had to put on a pace to get to the Houses of Parliament. The bustling crowds of London would have also added to his frustration and as Bellingham at last entered the courtyard of the House he would have been breathing heavily and with his heavy coat around him, sweat would have covered his brow.

Parliament had gathered to discuss the Orders in Council which were causing so much controversy in the country. The number of members present in the chamber was less than 70 of the 658 elected. Henry Brougham, a forceful reformer and frequent speaker in debates, was on his feet questioning Robert Hamilton. He was in the pottery trade at Stoke and a witness who was angry at the Orders in Council that he believed was destroying his business. In the Lobby of the House around twenty-five people were milling about in the usual commotion of parliamentary coming and goings. The hum of conversations between MP and constituent and lobbyists filled the air. William Smith, the MP for Norwich, entered the Lobby to make his way into the Chamber for the debate. He stopped to speak with Francis Phillips, who was a fellow anti-slave activist. Henry Burgess, a solicitor by profession, stood by the entrance doors of the House. He intended to grab the attention of the Prime Minister when he arrived. John Bellingham entered the Lobby and placed himself close to the same doors. Now in the Lobby at 4.45, he was anxious as he knew Perceval had been due to arrive at 4.30. He would have been relieved to hear the conversations around him, confirming Perceval was late. He relaxed in the knowledge that he had not lost his opportunity. John Norris, who worked at the House of Commons, passed by him and noted him 'to be anxiously watching'. Michael Saxton, a journeyman bookseller, stood near the entrance, also awaiting the arrival of Perceval. Away from the Lobby, in the various committee rooms, other members of the House attended their own business. One of these was acquainted with Bellingham; General Gascoyne, who was oblivious to his presence in the Lobby. To all intent and purposes, it was just an ordinary day in the House of Commons.

Spencer Perceval had left his Downing Street home. He was in no hurry; the business of the House was another attempt to divert him from his God-given conviction on the matter of the Orders in Council. This was the second occasion that necessitated his attendance as he had not turned up for the previous session as agreed. His lateness for the debate had prompted a messenger to be sent to hurry him along and so with a little more urgency, he moved forward and mounted the steps of the House and entered the Lobby. His tardiness at not being there promptly would turn out to be fatal. William Jerdan, a reporter with the British Press, became aware that the Prime Minister was behind him. He stepped aside to allow Perceval to precede him. In the hustle and bustle of the place his entrance was relatively unnoticed, except by John Bellingham who had been waiting for this moment. He stepped forward and removed the concealed pistol from the special pocket. In seconds, a ball of lead left the pistol and lodged deep in Perceval's heart. As he fell to the ground, the sound of the shot brought great commotion to those around. Richard Taylor the door-keeper lost his usual composure and a large number of people flooded into the Lobby from the Chamber, the House of Lords and the street. Gascoyne heard the shot and rushed down from the committee room where he had been sitting.

Perceval's body examined after the assassination.

Bellingham calmly walked away towards the fireplace. On a bench to one side of it he sat down. For him this was not an assassination – it was the execution of justice. He would have his day in Court – a day when he would appeal to the world and he would receive his justification and compensation. Although described as 'cool and collected', his face had gained a pallid complexion and large beads of sweat ran down from his forehead. His breathing was heavy and gave the appearance of choking him. He beat the palm of his hand against his chest to relieve the pressure. One watcher observed, 'Never on earth, I believe, was seen a more terrible example of over-wrought suffering.' Mr Eastaff, a clerk in the vote office, pointed to Bellingham, 'That is the man!'.

Within moments, he was surrounded by a group of anguished and angry men. Roughly handled, his shirt and coat were torn to expose his chest. Henry Burgess took hold of the pistol that Bellingham had left lying beside him on the bench, although Bellingham later thought he had taken it from his hand. It was still warm to the touch. He asked him, 'What could induce you to do such a deed?' to which he replied, 'Want of redress of grievance and a refusal by Government'; or words to that effect, according to Burgess. He was also asked if he had another pistol and was it also fully loaded to which he replied in the affirmative. Vincent Dowling, who was also in the House and had coming running down from the Gallery at the sound of the shot, found the second fully loaded pistol that was secreted under his clothes and removed it. He and William Jerdan took hold of Bellingham. They were joined by Burgess in searching him and removed a 'powerful opera glass in a red case', a golden guinea, a one-pound note, one bank token for 5s 6d and two for 1s 6d. They also removed a small pen-knife, a bunch of keys and a pencil. There was no sign of a prayer book that Bellingham had told Mrs Robarts he was buying.

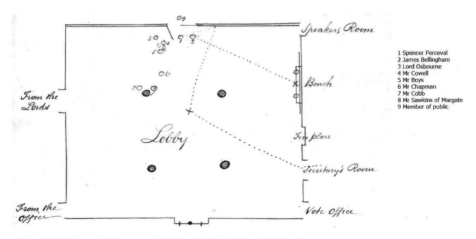

1 Spencer Perceval
2 James Bellingham
3 Lord Osbourne
4 Mr Cowell
5 Mr Boys
6 Mr Chapman
7 Mr Cobb
8 Mr Sawkins of Margate
9 Member of public

Sketch of House of Commons Lobby Made in May 1812.

Gascoyne was grasping him so tightly that he almost broke his wrist and he wrestled with Bellingham over a bundle of papers tied in red cloth tape that Bellingham had on his person. Bellingham was desperate not to lose these. They were the records of the injustices he had suffered and the many claims he had made. The papers were eventually taken from him and handed to Joseph Hume, MP for Weymouth, who had rushed from the Chamber at the sound of the gunfire. He sealed them with his seal and they were delivered to Castlereagh. Bellingham had said to Gascoyne, 'You need not press me, I submit to your justice.' Gascoyne also gave a different version of how the pistol was recovered from Bellingham. He said that he had wrestled the pistol from Bellingham after dramatically 'springing' on him and grasping his breast and neck. He then 'twisted his [Bellingham's] arm with all his force' to get the pistol. This was perhaps to embellish his own part, as he would have arrived at the scene later than Burgess. Gascoyne said he informed Bellingham that he could not escape, to which he replied, 'I am the person who shot Mr Perceval and I surrender myself.' Gascoyne also recounted meeting him and considered him, 'as calm and collected as any man could be, and had not the least appearance of a person insane'. Joseph Hume, a Member of Parliament on hearing Gascoyne's account could not be sure about how the pistol was recovered. He also affirmed that Bellingham, whilst agitated for a moment, was 'perfectly sane'.

Meanwhile, Perceval had been removed from the Lobby to the Speaker's room. When he had been shot he had staggered forward towards William Smith, who had stayed in the Lobby. His words were weak and thought to be 'Murder! Oh my God!' before he collapsed to the floor. It was only when he was turned over that Smith and Francis Phillips realised it was the Prime Minister. He was carried into the Speaker's room by them and they sat him at a table, supporting him from either side. There was a slight blood trickle from his mouth and barely a pulse. He gave a few weak convulsive sobs for three or four minutes. Although his eyes were open there was no response or movement. When all signs of life had gone, they felt for a pulse – there was none. They assumed he was dead and laid him down on top of the table. William Lynn, a surgeon who lived nearby was sent for. He noted the blood-stained white waistcoat and on examination 'a wound on the skin, about over left side, near the breast bone had the appearance of a large pistol ball having entered'. He could do nothing. Spencer Perceval, the Prime Minister, was officially declared dead.

A messenger from the Speaker's room returned to the chaos in the Lobby and announced to one and all, but especially Bellingham:

> 'Mr Perceval is dead! Villain! How could you destroy so good a man, and make a family of ten or twelve children orphans?'
> 'I am sorry for it. I am the unfortunate man – I wish I were in Mr Perceval's place. My name is John Bellingham; it is a private injury – I know what I have done. It was a denial of justice on the part of Government.'

As the scene calmed down a little, it was decided to bring Bellingham to the bar of the House of Commons, were the MPs reconvened. It was then that General Gascoyne, who had apparently not heard what was said in the Lobby, approached Bellingham to ask, 'Is your name not Bellingham?' Bellingham did not answer him but shook his head and then, motionless and apparently composed, rested his hands on a chair and stared directly at the Speaker's chair. The Speaker, now in a situation never met before by the House, proposed that he be removed to the Prison Room. There was great concern that Bellingham had not acted alone so it was therefore decided to avoid the Lobby and go through the private passages of the House. As a further precaution, some Members were chosen to precede the prisoner and witnesses in case of attack from anyone lying in wait. Magistrates from among the MPs were asked to question Bellingham and witnesses.

It was ascertained that an unnamed individual stood between Bellingham and Perceval and he had to raise his pistol above that individual in order to assassinate his quarry. Others recounted that they had seen Bellingham in the Gallery of the House and standing at the door noting MPs as they entered and left. Gascoyne informed them of his contact with Bellingham and the story of Russia and attempts to claim compensation. In turn, Bellingham maintained 'the utmost composure'. He told the gathering that he had 'watched for more than a fortnight for a favourable opportunity to effect his purpose'. He declared he had 'implored for justice in vain' and 'had made application to every person likely to procure him redress'. He, he argued, had been driven to despair:

> '… by being told at the public offices that he might do his worst – I have obeyed them, I have done my worst and I rejoice in my deed … I have admitted the fact—I admit the fact, but wish, with permission, to state something in my justification I have been denied the redress of my grievances by Government, I have been ill-treated They all know who I am, and what I am, though the Secretary of State and Mr. Beckett, with whom I have had frequent communications. They knew of this fact six weeks ago, though the magistrates of Bow Street. I was accused most wrongfully by a Governor General in Russia, in a letter from Archangel to Riga, and have sought redress in vain. I am a most unfortunate man, and feel here (placing his hand on his breast) sufficient justification for what I have done.'

Lord Castlereagh interrupted him to state that he was not being asked to defend himself and he should wait for his trial:

> 'Since it seems best to you that I should not now explain the causes of my conduct, I will leave it until the day of my trial, when my country will have the opportunity of judging whether I am right or wrong.'

He further repeated, 'I admit the fact'. There was no sense of confusion with him and as the Bow Street officers were called in to take charge, he asked for the money that had been taken from him after the assassination. He was given the assurance that he would receive it the next day. He also asked for an attorney and counsel and was again assured that these would be provided. There was no agitation with him or any sign of emotion. However, when a witness stated, 'I supported Mr Perceval into the secretary's room, and in a few minutes, he died in my arms', Bellingham shed tears and 'was much affected'. At one point, he also found fault with Vickery, the Bow Street officer, 'for having inquired from some female [Mrs Robarts] something relative to his private affairs'. Vickers calmly said that he knew the consequences of the act he had committed, which he did not consider 'a private affair'. Bellingham was told the conversation was in general terms and she had said she had a 'memorandum of £20' due from a Mr Wilson to him. He responded that he knew what it was and it was a bill he expected to be paid at nine thirty the next day. He also said he had no concerns and expected to be justified and set at liberty and to have his claims satisfied. Even now, after such a dreadful and shocking event, Bellingham remained implacable in his belief that he would be exonerated and still harboured belief in receiving compensation.

The Horse Guard, City Militia and the Foot Guard were all summoned onto the streets to protect Parliament and the peace of the city. The Houses of Parliament's windows and doors were all sealed as the crowd thronged the streets until after midnight. Instructions were dispatched throughout the land to ensure order was maintained. Not everyone was grieved at the death of Perceval, with many celebrating Bellingham's actions. They were not solely from the disadvantaged and poor, but in the drawing rooms of many of the powerful, affected by Perceval's decisions in Parliament, there was a quiet satisfaction at his removal.

Bellingham was taken from the House under strong guard and as he was conveyed to the coach to carry him to Newgate Prison, there were attempts to rescue him. The mob was calling the troops murderers rather than Bellingham. They heaped derision on the MPs in their carriages, who had to flee to more quiet streets to avoid their rage. One report stated:

> 'A person was arrested in Westminster for saying that he did not think there had been a man left in England that had the heart, alluding to the murderer of Mr Perceval, and that he could not shoot a greater rascal adding, "I'll fire my gun off tomorrow" …'

That was not the least of the authorities' concerns. In Nottingham and Leicester riots broke out in support of Bellingham, A flood of letters was written by many of which the following is an example:

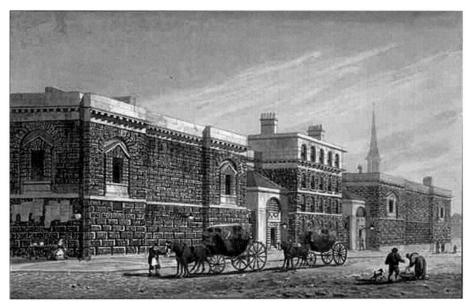

West View of Newgate by George Shepherd (1784-1862).

'May 12, 1812 Vox Populi
    'Addressed to Colonel Mc Mahon, Carlton-House, Pall Mall
    'George Prince of Wales take care of yourself for your Life is in danger,
you shall meet the same fate as Mr Perceval if Bellingham is hung before
this reach you. You blackguard! You shall be shot before three months is
elapsed if Bellingham is hung. You shall be shot as sure as I remain an
Enemy to all the damned Royal Family.'

Arriving at Newgate Prison, Bellingham was taken to a secure strong room under
the care of John Addison Newman, the head keeper. He and two guards spent the
night in the room with Bellingham. All over London the assassination reports had
spread to varying degrees of exaggeration and embellishment. The great and the
good at their dinner parties expressed their alarm. There were the many stories from
those 'who were there' but who in reality had no first-hand experience of the events.
They were all however, 'grateful that the military were on the streets all night'.
Many went from door to door to recount their tales; the whole of London was in
turmoil. In the House of Lords there was consternation. *Cobbett's Weekly Political
Register* on 23 May 1812 noted the reaction of the Lord Chancellor. Speaking to his
fellow 'Noble Lords', he trusted that they would give him credit, when he declared:

    '... that the state of the country was such, that it was necessary that the
    House should sit from day to day, in order to be ready to take such steps

as circumstances might require, for it was impossible to say what might happen in the course of a few days. It was his firm conviction, that such was the state of the country, that rendered it impossible for him to assent to any proposition for the placing the House in any other situation, than that of sitting from day to day.'

Bellingham was given some refreshments after which he calmly laid himself down on his bed and slept soundly, a most contented man.

The death of Perceval had naturally brought great pain and sorrow to his wife and children, one of whom (a 12-year-old) was reportedly in the House at the time of the killing. The body of Perceval was moved to Downing Street, sometimes through hostile crowds, which in turn caused diversions of the carriage carrying the body. Then there was the inquest which saw the witnesses give their accounts as noted above and the declaration by Dr William Lynn that:

'John Bellingham alias John Billingham not | having the fear of God before his Eyes but moved and seduced by the instigation of the Devil ... did make an Assault [with] a certain Pistol of the value of nine shillings charged and loaded with gunpowder and a leaden bullet ... and of his Malice aforethought did then and there give unto him the said Spencer Perceval with the leaden bullet aforesaid ... shot off and discharged out of the Pistol aforesaid by the force of the gunpowder aforesaid in upon and through the Breast of him the said Spencer Perceval one mortal wound ...'

Arrangements were made by the Lords and MPs to look after Perceval's family financially and ensure the schooling of his children. MPs and royalty were concerned that the assassination was the trigger for further uproar in the kingdom. Many of the ordinary populace were delighted with it, hoping that better days were ahead. The drawing rooms of the high and mighty were filled with conversations over the tea cups as to where it was all going and if they were safe in their beds. Liverpool authorities were embarrassed when the home city of Bellingham became known; steps were taken to visit his home and secure any evidence and statements from his wife, business partners and friends. Bow Street officers under the command of John Vickery were sent to his lodgings at New Millman Street to take charge of any papers and evidence of Bellingham's activities. In his room, they found bags that had contained the pistols, a gunpowder flask, a small box of gunpowder, four bullets in a bag, some flints and a pistol key wrapped in paper and a mould for casting bullets. The Government was in a state of shock and were anxious about his motives, asking that enquires be made about accomplices. Throughout London, and further afield, as news spread of the event, the question of the madness of the assailant were raised. It was thought by many that no sane man could have ever carried out such an atrocity.

Chapter 11

I Have Only Done My Duty

As this is a portrait of Bellingham, the assassin, we leave the turmoil he had created and focus on him as Tuesday dawned in Newgate prison. It was around 7 o'clock in the morning when he awoke from what was described as 'a peaceful sleep'. He was very relaxed and calm as he asked for breakfast from the head keeper, Newman, who was concerned that someone might attempt to poison Bellingham, so he prepared a large pot of sweetened tea himself. As he ate with his keepers, Bellingham was in a very happy mood. He told them where he was born and that he had a wife and three children in Liverpool. He chatted about what the newspapers were saying about him and corrected what he felt was wrong in the reporting. His whole demeanour belied the events of the previous day.

The visit by Mr Alderman Combe and some other magistrates to question him was very cordial and respectful from both parties. He also asked them about the assassination and how the ball had entered Perceval's chest. When they informed him of the downward travel of the ball and that it was speculated that he had fired over a bystander's shoulder, he was shocked. He doubted the scenario of someone being anywhere in the line of fire and being endangered. He declared he would never have fired if Perceval had not been directly before him. A Mr Hokkirk tried to be admitted but was refused; he declared to the keepers that Bellingham's father was deranged and that Bellingham himself was also mad. Similar ideas were being reported in the press, however, these reports, in the main, struggled to reconcile how insanity could be true as it was known that Bellingham was calm and collected, that he had conducted business regularly and normally. He had also written many letters and conducted a series of communications which all indicated a sound mind.

Bellingham never expressed any sense of guilt at his actions, nether had he any remorse for what he had done. To anyone who would listen, he made it clear that all he sought was justice and redress for the wrongs against him. Had he not been driven to despair by the refusal of anyone to listen and give to him what he was due? Had not the representatives of government given him permission for his actions, telling him to do whatever he thought necessary to bring his case before the courts and public? Such thinking was at the root of his assassination of Perceval. In his mind it was neither abnormal, nor insane but the logical step he had to take. He had a genuine belief that his day in court would be his day of justification.

He wrote letters to Mrs Robarts, Mary and John Parton. The letter to his landlady gives us insight into his mind:

'Tuesday morning. Old Bailey
'Dear Madam,
    'Yesterday midnight I was escorted to this neighbourhood by a noble troop of light horse, and delivered into the care of Mr Newman (by Mr Taylor, the magistrate and MP) as a State Prisoner of the first class. For eight years I have never found my mind so tranquil as since this melancholy, but necessary catastrophe: as the merits or demerits of my peculiar case must be regularly unfolded in a Criminal Court of Justice to ascertain the guilty party, by a jury of my country, I have to request the favour of you to send me three or four shirts, some cravats, handkerchiefs, night-caps, stockings, &c. out of my drawers, together with comb, soap, toothbrush, with any other trifle that presents itself which you think I may have occasion for, and inclose them in my leather trunk, and the key please to send sealed, per bearer; also my great coat, flannel gown, and black waistcoat, which will much oblige, Dear Madam, your very obedient Servant,
                                JOHN BELLINGHAM
To the above please to add the prayer book.'

Here he reveals his need to be esteemed and treated as important. He is 'a State Prisoner of the first class'. For eight years he has pursued his cause with despair, anger, agitation and frustration, but now his mind is 'tranquil'. The assassination itself was not a random thoughtless action; it was a 'necessary catastrophe' – necessary because it had to go to public court and a jury, who, as we have seen already, he believed would find him innocent. He then asks to be sent the items that will allow him to appear in public in the most presentable way. His post script is strange. For a man who has just committed brutal murder and has shown no remorse, guilt or repentance, he wants the comfort of a prayer book. He believed his conscience was clear and he had executed his own justice.

By the Wednesday, the government were becoming more settled that Bellingham had acted alone. The issue of his madness needed clarification and it would be inconvenient for them if he was determined to be insane. They would wish for a quick trial and execution as a lesson to anyone else who harboured thoughts of rebellion. The newspapers now had had time to gather information and their reports were filled with details, sometimes wrong, about Bellingham. However, as he awoke at 7am and enjoyed a light breakfast, he was again in conversation with his keepers. He had been supplied with a few newspapers, which he took delight in reading. He was particularly pleased to see in print his memorial giving his account of how he came to be where he was:

'My memorial then has at last gone forth to the world; the public will now be
able to judge my case and do me the justice to say I have only done my duty'

His keepers were unhappy with his attitude and rebuked him for his remarks.
However, he was totally indifferent to them; he seemed not to care about his
situation or what would happen to him. It appeared that he had now come to terms
with his experiences in Russia and his treatment on returning to England. He was
certain that he had done the right thing in assassinating Perceval, as it was the
only way he could right the wrongs done to him. His arrogance was apparent as he
declared they could 'do no harm' to him and indeed it was the 'Government who
had cause to fear'.

Bellingham was at the centre of attention and that day he had many visitors, the
sheriffs, among others, who wanted to understand what motivated him. He was
quite content to talk reasonably and in a calm and considered manner, except when
the subject turned to the assassination. Here he became animated and agitated,
insisting that he would be vindicated in his actions. He was determined to point
out that the public would understand that he was an injured individual and that
people would discover how far a minister was justified in refusing justice to him.
His argument that he had not shot the man but the minister and that he would be
'worse than a brute' if he had acted with any sort of personal malice.

His solicitor, James Harmer, made a visit and spent some two hours discussing
the defence case. Harmer was a portly man, very Dickensian in appearance; indeed,
many years later, he was to become the inspiration behind Mr Jaggers, a character
in Dickens' *Great Expectations*. He was the son of a Spitalfields weaver, and was left
an orphan at age 10; in this, he would be sympathetic to Bellingham. He was articled
to an attorney in 1792 and transferred from private practice to Messrs. Fletcher
& Wright of Bloomsbury, and returned to practise for himself in 1799. He had a
reputation for representing radicals and underdogs. He was quite expert in the law
and meticulous in dealing with appointed barristers. There is no doubt Bellingham
had the benefit of a very able solicitor. Harmer read as extensively as he could on
the background of his client and in his conversation with Bellingham, he found a
man assured of his acquittal and vindication. Indeed, he was triumphant and sure
that when the people understood how he had been treated and denied justice, there
would be no question that he had acted rightly. It would be seen that he had been
forced to kill Perceval; it was not murder but an act of justice. Harmer had to press
home to him the need that a legal defence would still have to be made. He finally
persuaded him to give names of those who could appear as witnesses for the defence.
On leaving Bellingham, Harmer immediately wrote urgent correspondence to
Liverpool. Letters were addressed to the Mayor of Liverpool and John Parton. He
also wrote to Ann Billet now living in Southampton. He knew that because there

was no question his client had fired the shot that killed the Prime Minister, the only case that could me made was that he was insane when he carried out the action. He believed he could prove that Bellingham was obviously obsessive and any jury would consider him delusional, as we have already discussed, to the point of insanity.

Harmer was not the only one to consider the question of insanity. The files in the Treasury records show that the prosecution was aware that this was the only line the defence could reasonably take. They therefore had prepared by reviewing the case of Rex v Arnold; as we will see later, the prosecution argument from this case would be well made. Its basic premise was that the 'shooting was malicious' and 'dependent on the sanity of the man'. The aspect to the question of sanity was further based on the man having the 'use of his reason and sense'. However, as W.S. Holdsworth pointed out, in citing a speech by the notable advocate Erskine in 1800, that even a true lunatic could still be declared sane if it was proven that he was able to distinguish right from wrong. This then at the time of Bellingham's trial was the key question; did he know what he was doing and could he distinguish between good and evil? Harmer sat out to prove that his judgement was so affected by his treatment in Russia and England, that his obsession robbed him of those abilities. He called on Dr Thomas Munroe and Dr Samuel Simmons to testify to the insanity of his client. Munroe had unsuccessfully given evidence in a case where a severely war damaged veteran had fired a pistol at George III, believing the king's death would bring in the new millennium. Simmons had attended the king in his periods of madness. Harmer also hoped to bring Ann Billet and John Parton to confirm Bellingham's insanity. The newspapers too were filled with columns as to his mental state. There was great confusion in the debate. For many there was no doubt that he was insane; how could any sane man kill and act afterwards the way he had done? However, there were others who pointed to his behaviour as a business man and argued that an insane man could not have conducted business the way he did. Some even carried examples of his handwriting arguing that such a style was not that of a madman.

On Thursday, Bellingham arose at his usual time and was reported to be refreshed and apparently still unaffected by the assassination he had carried out. He breakfasted at 8.30 and then the morning was spent pacing his cell, slightly

Example of Bellingham's writing.

hampered by his chained ankles. He had a prayer book in his hand which he would occasionally read. He dined at 2 o'clock on minced veal and potatoes, washed down with a jug of porter. On that morning at the Session House, Clerkenwell, the Grand Jury assembled to decide on an indictment. Under foreman David Owen, himself a merchant, twenty-two other business citizens of London heard witnesses once more give their statements of what they witnessed at the House of Commons. They then concluded that they had found 'a true Bill against John Bellingham, for the wilful murder of the Right Honourable Spencer Perceval'. Their next step was to

The Session House, Clerkenwell.

attend at the Court of Oyer and Terminer at Justice Hall in the Old Bailey and declare their findings. The Treasury files show the indictment that was drawn up with many corrections to ensure the wording was indeed correct. In an unusual step, Charles Litchfield, the Solicitor for the Treasury, went to Newgate Prison and personally told Bellingham of the indictment. The rush to trial was obvious; it was to be the next day Friday, 15 May.

This does raise the question of due process and a fair trial. Harmer, his solicitor, had just been appointed. The issuing of letters to summon witnesses would take time. Indeed, because of the many letters Bellingham had written that brought Russia into the matter, there needed to be time for gathering evidence for the defence. In any other trial, it would be reasonable for the defence to have two to five weeks for this purpose. The speed demonstrates the urgency of government interfering in the legal procedure; they wanted a quick trial to demonstrate to any other potential associates of Bellingham or other malcontents that there would be swift and decisive action against them. Their belief was that the outcome of the trial would be a guilty verdict and the execution of Bellingham certain.

Another visitor was Mary Stevens, who was heading back to Liverpool that day and decided on a last visit. She thought the visit would give Bellingham an opportunity to write to his wife, but 'he would rather wait till the next day, that he might acquaint her with his liberation, which he confidently anticipated before the post going out'. This helps to understand Bellingham's inner belief in his actions as a matter of justice. He is adamant that what has happened would be seen by the jury as natural and right. Does this suggest that Bellingham is mad in the sense he is displaying a delusional disorder? Whilst there, Stevens witnessed Bellingham receiving a box containing seventy pounds in bank notes and other coinage to the total of 100 guineas (£12,000). The source these funds was unknown but it was generally thought at the time it was to aid his defence. It may also reflect the fact that there were some who supported his action.

At around four o'clock his solicitor arrived and Bellingham indicated he would look after his own affairs and would not have any further discussion. Here again we touch on Bellingham's inner being. In his mind, he does not want a third party managing his defence. He needs to be able to convince everyone of his right to take his own means of justice, just as he believed he had been told by the authorities. To this end, after 6 o'clock he had some tea and then sat down to the job of writing out his own defence arguments. By nine he had exhausted his supply of paper and asked Newman the keeper for more. He also asked for some wine. Only the paper was supplied. In custom with prison practice, his trunk of belongings was removed whilst he kept the key to its contents. He retained his dressing gown and after a jug of porter he returned to his writing. He retired at midnight but was awake again at 3am and made more notes. After that, he returned to bed and slept soundly until seven.

Chapter 12

I Put Myself Upon God and My Country

On Friday 15 May 1812, Bellingham was awake at his usual hour. Once more, he was reported to be in a state of great calmness. He was attended to by a hairdresser who cut his hair very short and provided him with a clean shave. There was no randomness in the clothing he chose. He wore dark nankeen trousers, made from Chinese cotton, with a yellow waistcoat that had small black stripes. Over this he wore a brown greatcoat and to all observers he was the perfect gentleman. He had been examined by William Box the Newgate Prison surgeon and passed as fit to be tried at the Old Bailey. It was noted that around breakfast time of 8.30 he began to show some signs of stress. He ate little of the food provided and at one point burst into tears. The concerned keepers were assured by him that the tears were not for his own plight bur for that of his wife and children and the position he in which he had placed them. This gives a clue to Bellingham and how he behaved. In Liverpool he had been seething within with anger and resentment and a determination to get back to London to continue his fight, yet on the outward appearance, attested by those around him, he was calm and in control. In Newgate Prison, the continuous reports were also of a calm and contented man, yet here the inner man broke through to the surface and betrayed that not all about him may be what it seemed. He asked for an orange and after eating it seemed to return to full composure. He sat and penned a letter headed, 'Old Bailey May 15th 1812'. It was to his business partner in Liverpool, Parton. He told Parton that he had probably by now heard of the 'melancholy catastrophe that had befallen Mr Perceval'. He then went on to make his claim that it was 'in consequence of the repeated refusal of justice'. The result was that he 'could stand it no longer' and resolved to bring the matter to a criminal court, where he believed that he would be vindicated. Indeed, if he was right, 'no one would be able to touch a hair on his head'. He was anxious to get to court stating, 'the sooner it can be done the more agreeable to me'. There is still a streak of arrogance or aspects of his delusion when he again describes himself as, 'a state prisoner of the first class'. He acknowledges he has been given every comfort and convenience and since the whole 'Russian business' started he has never felt so much 'tranquillity'. He is confident that everything will be 'unfolded' and the 'unprecedented persecution' will be 'for ever at rest'. He informs Parton that he has not written to his wife because she will not be able to

IOHN BELLINGHAM,
the
ASSASSIN.

Mr. A. Newman
Keeper of Newgate

Drawn by Permission in Court by W. Medland

A sketch of Bellingham done at the trial.

handle it as her 'constitution' had not the same ability and calmness of his own; Parton was therefore to show her the contents of this letter. He asked Parton to send him any papers that may be relevant to the Russian business and ends with 'affectionate remembrances to my wife and boys, whom I hope to embrace with joy after this bitter cup of affliction shall have passed over'. With this hope of being freed, he would now face that criminal court. When it was time, Head Keeper Newman led him through the various passages that led from Newgate to the Session House. Here he would give an account of his affairs and as has been noted, he had the firm conviction he would leave the court a free man.

The *Globe* reported that crowds had started to gather outside the Court at 7am. Entrance was only allowed for those who had a written order from the Sheriffs. However, some were turned away because they refused to pay the high prices – unauthorised – demanded by the doorkeepers; they were charging between one and three guineas (£65-£195). About 2,000 people remained in the street, curious to see the comings and goings of the trial. Around 10 o'clock, Sir James Mansfield, Mr. Justice Grote and Mr. Barron Graham, came to sit on the bench. Also, there were the Lord Mayor and a number of the Aldermen. The Duke of Clarence, Richard Wellesley and others also attended. In other parts of the court, the members of parliament who were subpoenaed as witnesses sat. Close to them were the Earl of Uxbridge, Sir Arthur Paget, Lord Gower, Sir Francis Burdett and many more of the MPs and grandees of London. Bellingham had wanted his day in court and now before him sat many of the men he believed had ignored and ill-used him. The prosecution would be led by the Attorney General, Sir Vicary Gibbs, an unpopular politician with a reputation for being 'caustic' in the Courtroom. He would be assisted by William Garrow and others.

Immediately on the Judges taking their places, John Bellingham was called to the dock. On his entrance to the court some papers reported he looked shocked as he saw the crowd but he recovered quickly as he took his place in the dock.

The *Newgate Calendar* recorded him as 'advancing with a firm step, quite undismayed. He bowed to the Court most respectfully and even gracefully'. The *Globe* among other papers called him shabbily dressed, which revealed more of their prejudice than the truth. The *Calendar* again noted:

> 'It is impossible to describe the impression which his appearance, accompanied by this unexpected fortitude, produced. He was dressed in a light brown surtout coat, and striped yellow waistcoat; his hair plainly dressed, and without powder [which was the more accurate].'

Sir Vicary Gibbs.

The important point for this character portrait is that he looked every inch a normal sane man, who was perfectly composed.

However, as we continue to look at the portrait of the assassin we find that he had already accepted that he killed Perceval but he would raise his defence on the idea of it not being with *malice prepense* (malice aforethought). This was the idea of an action, wrong or injury purposely done. At the conclusion of his defence he would burst into tears and stated:

> 'If, whenever I am called before the tribunal of God, I can appear with as clear a

A contemporary sketch of Bellingham at the trial.

conscience as I now possess in regard to the alleged charge of the wilful
murder of the unfortunate Gentleman, the investigation of whose death has
occupied your attention, it would be happy for me, as essentially securing
to me eternal salvation – but that is impossible That my arm has been the
means of his melancholy and lamented exit, 1 am ready to allow. But to
constitute murder, it must clearly and absolutely be proved to have arisen
from *malice prepense*, and with a malicious design, as I have no doubt the
Learned Judge will shortly lay down, in explaining the law on the subject.
If such is the case, I am guilty – if not, I look forward with confidence to
your acquittal'

This was the statement that summarises Bellingham's inner belief. He held two
things in tension; he had killed Spencer Perceval, but he had not murdered him.
This is a classic condition that is seen in modern psychology – cognitive dissonance.
That is to say, a person may have a sincere belief but also be involved in an action
that is in disagreement with that belief. With Bellingham, he had a belief – murder
was wrong under God's law – but he carried out an action – he murdered – against
God's law. This conflict is the likely reason why he became distressed and wept. The
need to maintain cognitive consistency, that is to balance the belief with the action,
is a powerful motive that can give rise to irrational and sometimes maladaptive
behaviour. Therefore, Bellingham would strive to convince himself and others, that
his action was not murder but the consequence of a pursuit of justice. With this,
the pain of the dissonance would be relieved. Combine this with the symptoms of
delusion he had presented and we see a man under extreme emotional turmoil.
Having this in mind, we can now follow his journey to the conclusion of the trial.

When Mr. Alley intervened, at the start of the trial, as Bellingham was called on to
plead to the indictment, he argued that the trial should be postponed because of the
absence of witnesses who were material to the prisoner's defence. It was necessary
to allow time to provide proof of his client's insanity. It seemed a reasonable request
as the trial had been brought forward so quickly. Alley was not allowed to proceed
and the indictment was read and the usual question, "Guilty, or not guilty?' was put
to Bellingham. When he addressed the Court he too was unhappy:

'My Lords, before I can plead to this indictment, I must state, in justice
to myself, that by hurrying on my trial I am placed in a most remarkable
situation. It so happens that my prosecutors are actually the witnesses
against me. All the documents on which alone I could rest my defence
have been taken from me, and are now in possession of the crown. It is only
two days since I was told to prepare for my defence and when 1 asked for
my papers, I was told they could not be given up. It is therefore, my lords,
rendered utterly impossible for me to go into mv justification and under
the circumstances in which I find myself, a trial is absolutely useless. The

papers are to be given to me after the trial, but how can that avail me for my defence? I am, therefore, not ready for my trial'

There then followed a furious dialogue between the prosecution and defence on the matter of the case not proceeding until the defendant gave an answer to the question of his guilt. The Attorney General was caught wrong footed by Bellingham's argument on his papers. The prosecution demanded that the defence not be allowed to speak until a plea was made. The Chief Justice brought the argument back to the question of the plea. That had to be settled before the court could move forward. Bellingham was reluctant to plea until the matter of his papers was resolved. However, the insistence of the court won out and he was forced to respond. Still unhappy, in a quiet voice he finally responded, 'Not Guilty. I put myself upon God and my country.'

The Attorney General, having had his feathers ruffled, tried to regain his footing by explaining the papers had been withheld in order to serve justice but the prisoner had been informed that if the solicitor requested them then would be supplied for the trial. However, he was again reproved by the defence that that had only happened the day before the trial. He therefore asked to make a speech to the court on the defendant's insanity but the prosecution objected that the rules forbade such a thing. He cited the case of Rex v Arnold already referred to, in which counsel for the defence was refused permission to make any statements on the defendant's insanity; this was upheld. Mr Alley therefore was only allowed to read two affidavits into the Court. The first was from Bellingham's cousin and childhood friend, Ann Billet. It stated that she had known Bellingham for many years and that he lived in Liverpool. She stated that there were many people like herself who could be called to testify to his insanity if there were time. She also referred to Captain Barker of the Militia who was a material witness and would be able to confirm that Bellingham had demonstrated insanity for some time – Barker was one of the arbitrators in Russia. The second affidavit was from Mary Clarke, who had known Bellingham for a few years and believed him to be insane. She also referred to the time needed for his relations to come from Liverpool to also confirm his insanity.

Alley followed these statements with a plea that 'it was only on Monday that the alleged act was said to have been perpetrated'. He pointed out that letters to Liverpool could only be sent the next day and it was impossible to believe that a response could have been received by the time the trial started. Even if the trial had been held in Liverpool, the same problems of time would be an issue. The Attorney General was in a hurry to get a verdict and immediately objected to the defence line on time. He dismissed it as 'clearly a contrivance to delay the administration of justice'. He then attacked the two women as complicit and specially chosen 'to impose on the Court a false belief'. He then challenged the justices as to their response if they delayed the proceedings, intimating that they would also be complicit. Indeed, 'the general purposes of justice ... will be grossly violated if your Lordships consent to the procrastination proposed.' He went on to claim that the two women had no knowledge of the state of Bellingham's mind in the last four months or at the time of the murder. Rather there was no one around who knew him at this time who could testify to his insanity. He then turned and directly attacked Ann Billet and Mary Clarke:

"None of these persons are called before your Lordships, to prove the state of his mind – none of those who knew and could have given evidence of the fact are brought before the Court but a contrivance is resorted to – one woman, coming up from Southampton, but generally residing in Dorsetshire, and another living in this city, make affidavits of the prisoner's insanity, but neither of them have attempted to swear, that he was in an infirm state of mind about the time the crime was committed'

The Attorney General was not finished. He now turned his fire on Mr Alley:

'I will call to your Lordships' recollection, what the Prisoner has just now addressed to the Court, and the studious anxiety manifested by his Counsel to prevent his making those observations which they conceived would influence the Court in coming to the decision that he was not insane, which was contrary to what they wished. If indeed, there was any ground for the plea of insanity, or of infirmity of mind, who is the best judge of it, and by whom could it be most satisfactorily proved? Would not his Counsel have sent a person, conversant in such disorders, to examine the Prisoner; some person whose statement your Lordships would have regarded as of deep importance? No such course has been pursued; but Affidavits, such as I have described, have been put in – evidently not to advance, but to retard and weaken justice. If, in the case of the meanest individual, you would grant the application founded on those Affidavits, let it be done in this but if it would be refused in other cases, I trust it will not be conceded, for the first time, now."

This slur on Mr. Alley's ability did not go unchallenged. He wished to answer the question put by the Attorney General. Alley said that he was only asking their Lordships to exercise that discretion which the law gave them, and to do to his client what they would do to others in a similar situation. As to why he did not get the necessary information and advice of some gentleman well conversant in those disorders was obvious; he had only received his instructions the previous evening. He and his co-counsel, Mr. Reynolds, had sought the assistance of two of the ablest and most celebrated men of the day, Doctors Simmons and Munro. One of them had said that it was impossible for him to appear this day, and the other had not yet answered. The defence counsel had taken these steps as a matter of duty. The speed of setting the trial was the problem. His client's wife and family were most likely to be acquainted with his infirmity; but they could not arrive in London in time. Under such circumstances, he asked the Court to grant the application on the basis of the affidavits then before them. Mr. Reynolds rose to support his defence colleague but was forbidden to speak by the Court Recorder. The defence had made a reasonable claim and it now rested on the justices to decide whether the trial should be postponed.

Their deliberation was short and they returned to give their answer to the defence. The defence had shown through the affidavits that indeed there was evidence that in the past their client had shown signs of possible insanity, particularly in Russia and on his return two years ago. However, no evidence had been produced to show that at the time of the criminal act or the months preceding it, he had been in a state of insanity. For the justices, this was the key point and therefore, in light of this, they could see no reason to delay the trial of Bellingham. Alley could only put on record his objection to the decision. This illustrates the lamentable state of the understanding of mental health issues at that time and the situation would never occur in modern law. The court then moved to empanel the jury. One prospective juror, Mr Samuel Brown, was peremptorily challenged by the crown and the defence objected as such challenges could only be made in cases of high treason. He was overruled and once more placed his objection on record.

With the indictment once more being read out, the Attorney General proceeded with his case. He knew he had to contrast the 'goodness' of Perceval with the 'evil' of Bellingham. He also had to ensure that the jury would not be allowed to see Bellingham as a man who was insane but a man who was rational and who had acted in revenge. Bellingham's act was 'a horrid murder'. He played to the goodness of Perceval who 'would have spent his last moment in uttering a prayer for the forgiveness of his murderer'. He went on to inform the jury that, 'the country has [had] torn from it its brightest ornament – but the country has done justice to his memory', the implication being that the jury too must now do justice to that same memory. Indeed, Perceval was 'an honourable, upright, worthy man'. Having spoken of these matters, he now told them they should not be swayed by them, though of course his intention was that they would be so swayed. It was to satisfy public justice and not revenge or resentment against the accused that should guide their decision. In the next breath, he refers to the prisoner 'who has committed this murder and assassination'. He then said he did not know the prisoner except in the circumstances that related to the case. There then was a recital of the details that by now were well known through the newspapers, of his time in Russia and his return to England. In the course of his transactions he had been found to be 'of sound mind', managing not just his own affairs but the affairs of others. He then cleverly sowed doubt in any claim by Bellingham that there was an injustice in Russia at the root of his claims:

> 'He went to Russia – and there, whether through his own misconduct or by the justice or injustice of that country, he was thrown into prison'

He referred to Gower's and Shairp's refusal to assist but would not discuss the whys and wherefores of that refusal. He then recounted Bellingham's attempts to get ministers to grant him compensation for his Russian treatment, saying that 'he seems to have cherished in his mind a feeling of the propriety of making an application to Government'. However, Ministers found them 'unworthy of attention' despite their being 'examined'. He spoke of the application to parliament and individual MPs. Spencer Perceval was his next avenue for redress but:

> 'Governed by those principles of justice, which always regulated and directed his conduct, he did not think it justified in acceding to his request, and he refused it'

Once more, it was Perceval who had acted justly, the inference being that Bellingham had not. Indeed, now came the true reason, according to the prosecution, for his action:

> 'From the moment that the Prisoner found that his Majesty's Ministers would not countenance his application to Parliament for what he chose to call, a remuneration for services rendered; at that moment the at that moment the desire for revenge arose in his mind, and from that same moment he resolved upon this dreadful act'

Here then was the real motive, according to the Attorney General; revenge not justice. He then outlined how Bellingham had set out in his resolution to complete the 'horrible purpose'. There was the purchasing of the pistols, the spying out of the movements of Perceval, the adding of the pocket to the coat and the choosing of the time to strike. The questions now were: is the 'man at the Bar the murderer or not?'; 'Whether he shall or shall not answer the justice of his country, for the act he performed?'; 'Is he guilty or is he not of this horrid murder, this foul assassination?' As for the Attorney General, he could 'see no reason to doubt' the answers. Now he turned to the defence's claim of insanity and their attempts to 'put off the trial'. For the purposes of the portrait of the assassin, let us look at the prosecution' view of the matter:

'Nothing remains but for the attempt that has been made this day to put off this Trial, upon the foolish and vain pretence, that the person at the bar is incapable of performing any act of sanity, or of managing with judgment any manner of business. Now let us consider this subject in its legal point of view. Has he not, as a man, been conducting himself like others in the ordinary affairs of life? Has he not been left to the management of his own concerns? No one of his family nor of his friends, have been interfering to control him in that management. There has been no just pretence alleged, that he was not capable of conducting them himself. On the contrary, he has not only been left free and uncontrolled in conducting his own concerns, but he has been employed in managing the affairs of others, by which they have displayed the judgment they entertained of his understanding. There appears, Gentlemen, to have been no blemish upon his understanding. What colour can be given for the Defence which I understand is to be set up, that this man was, as in law it is called, *non-compos mentis*, or that he was not an accountable being, I know not. He manages his own affairs in a manner that no person complains of, and he is entrusted with the management of the affairs of others. What is there to raise, not a presumption, but a pretence, a suspicion that he was not capable in his mind? I know well the principle upon which insanity is received as a defence; I know that the man to whom I should impute insanity, must be one that is incapable of malice because he is visited by that which, in the original signification of the word, means an absence of all mind by madness; I know that in such a case, were such a person to commit murder, I could not question his right to plead insanity by the Laws of his Country. Am I today to learn, that the wickedness of his conduct in committing the act with which he is charged, and for which he is called upon to answer with his life, is to be brought forward as a proof that he is not answerable for it?'

He then gave another contrived example of a man intending to carry out an assassination, to underline his point. If a man had acted rationally and normally throughout his life, an assassination may look mad but it does not remove his rationality. One act of insanity does not mean the man is insane. He continued to labour this idea:

'Were madness to be pleaded as an excuse in such cases as this, then every act of great atrociousness would carry its own defence within itself. Every man who committed a crime greater than the ordinary sort of criminality might set up as a defence, that it was impossible that any person could be guilty of such enormity, possessed of a sane or a proper understanding, or who was capable of judging whether the act was right or wrong.'

For the prosecution, this was an important point of law. Was Bellingham capable or incapable of distinguishing between right and wrong? they argued; 'for if he were capable of doing so, he is criminally responsible for such an enormous offence'. This is vital to the understanding of how Bellingham's character and state of mind was being viewed not only in the mind of the Attorney General but also in the mind of government. They had a vested interest in Bellingham being found sane, guilty and then executed as a deterrent to others. The caustic Vicary Gibbs decided to spell it out for the jury:

> 'It may be necessary, Gentlemen, that I should explain to you the difference between that state of insanity which would render a man's civil acts void, and that which would excuse him from responsibility for the commission of an offence which, in another man, would be criminal.'

He was making sure that when the defence rose to defend Bellingham by claiming he was in a state of insanity, he had already defeated their argument:

> 'A man may be deranged in his mind, his intellect maybe insufficient for enabling him to conduct the common affairs of life, disposing of his property, or judging of the claims which his respective relations have upon him and if he be so, the Administration of the country will take his affairs into their management, and appoint to him trustees but, at the same time, such a man is not discharged from his responsibility for criminal acts.'

Here he laid the grounds that even if Bellingham was not capable of handling his own affairs, and Vicary Gibbs would try to prove he was, Bellingham was still a responsible person. Then he had to make sure the jury were convinced not simply by his words but by the weight of the wisdom of legal history:

> 'I say this upon the authority of the first Sages in this country, and upon the authority of the established Law in all times, and which Law has never been questioned, that although a man be incapable of conducting his own affairs, he may still be answerable for his criminal acts, if he possess a mind capable of distinguishing right from wrong. In all cases that have hitherto been called in question in a Court of Law, the person whose conduct has been under consideration, has been in many respects found to be insane up to a certain period and the question has been, whether that insanity was such as to render him incapable of distinguishing right from wrong; and in many of those cases, although it were admitted that many acts of insanity had been committed by the prisoner whose conduct was then in question, yet, if he appeared to possess sufficient understanding to distinguish right from wrong, he was always made criminally answerable.'

There then was the nub of the Attorney General's final thrust. Whether it was thought that the assassination of Perceval was an act of madness in itself or if it was thought that Bellingham had at periods of his life demonstrated madness, as people like Ann Billet were claiming, there was no legal reason to suppose he was free from guilt for his actions. He underlined his legal opinion with two case law examples; Rex v Arnold and Rex v Lord Ferrers, who murdered Mr. Johnstone, his steward. In both cases, friends and relatives had tried to argue that both accused were insane because of their strange behaviour in normal life. In both cases, these arguments had been thrown out and guilty verdicts were issued as it was determined they were sane at the time of the murders. The Attorney General having laid his foundations for a guilty verdict built on them by calling the witnesses for the prosecution.

One by one, they took the stand and described their stories in dramatic detail. All made sure of their role at the centre of history. The testimonies of the witnesses do not need to be retold in detail. The simple truth was that every witness called by the defence gave uniformly the same story with small variances. Some had seen John Bellingham fire a pistol at Spencer Perceval and kill him. Others had witnessed the aftermath and the struggle with Bellingham. The doctor had examined the body and confirmed death by a pistol shot. John Vickery, the Bow Street officer, would confirm the incriminating evidence found at the defendant's rooms. James Taylor would recite the story of making the pocket for the raincoat. Testimony from others who knew him or looked after him at his lodgings would confirm him as a normal man who had never shown signs of deviant behaviour. It was a case in which there was no doubt that the defendant had assassinated the Prime Minister. Moreover, John Bellingham had readily accepted before many witnesses that he indeed had carried out the deed. Therefore, in this commonality of the testimonies there was no doubt in anyone's mind of one certainty; John Bellingham had shot Spencer Perceval and had planned it in detail.

Chapter 13

My Insanity Was Made a Matter of Public Notoriety

It was now Bellingham's turn to offer his defence. He rose from his seat and bowed respectfully to the court and spoke in 'a firm tone of voice'; however, it was so quiet that it was not totally heard by the Bench or the greater part of the court. He was instructed to speak directly to the jury. In appearance, he was described as 'no way embarrassed', nor did he display any emotion at the precarious situation in which he found himself. He addressed the jury:

> 'Gentlemen of the Jury, I feel great personal obligation to the Attorney General, for the objection which he has made to the plea of insanity. I think it is far more fortunate that such a plea as that should have been unfounded, than that it should have existed in fact. I am obliged to my Counsel however, for having thus endeavoured to consult my interest, as I am convinced the attempt has arisen from the kindest motives. That I am or have been insane is a circumstance of which I am not apprised, except in the single instance of my having been confined in Russia, where my insanity was made a matter of public notoriety. How far that may be considered as affecting my present situation, it is not for me to determine.'

The *Morning Chronicle* reported that at this point he became embarrassed and had to pause. In modern psychology, embarrassment is understood to result from potential negative evaluations by others, concerning standards about actions, thoughts, and feelings that govern behaviour. This is almost certain what was happening with Bellingham. His thoughts, feelings and actions were now going to be put on public display. This would no doubt be very difficult for the proud and indeed vain man that Bellingham had been found to be.

In trying to understand him, this opening statement offers up a number of questions. On one hand, it suggests that he does not accept that he is insane as a general condition but on the other he states that he is not able to determine whether that is true or not. There appears to be the acknowledgement that in Russia he may well have been insane, but as to how that insanity affected him at this time was an open question. There is also the idea that Bellingham is able to discuss rationally the question of his insanity. Does that in itself make him sane? What it surely must have done is reduce the chances of a jury of non-medical men considering him to be insane and thus guilty of a volitional act of murder.

Arising from his embarrassment, he informed the court that this was the first time he had addressed any public audience and asked them to listen to the detail of what he had to say rather than the way he delivered it. He then gave full admission to the 'crime which I have committed'. However, the deed was committed by a compulsion due to circumstances and not in any way voluntary or with 'any hostility to the man whom it has been my fate to destroy'. In one account of his speech, he calls himself a 'compulsive volunteer to this Bar'. He asked the jury if they thought him a man who would 'go with a deliberate design without cause or provocation with a pistol to put an end to the life of Mr Perceval?' Indeed, he declared:

> 'Considering the amiable character, and universally admitted virtues of Mr. Perceval, I feel, if I could murder him in a cool and unjustifiable manner I should not deserve to live another moment in this world. I have strong reasons for my conduct, however extraordinary; reason that when I have concluded you will acknowledge, to have fully justified me in this fatal fact. Had I not possessed these imperious incitements, and had murdered him in cold blood, I should consider myself a monster and not only unfit to live in this world but too wicked for all the torments that may be inflicted in the next.'

This was what Bellingham had always wanted – justification that would bring him compensation. He genuinely expected that when a jury heard his case then the outcome was certain – his freedom. He therefore continued:

> 'Conscious, however, that I shall be able to justify everything which I have done, I feel some degree of confidence in meeting the storm which assails me, and shall now proceed to unfold a catalogue of circumstances which will harrow up my own soul, will, I am sure, tend to the extenuation of my conduct in this honourable Court.'

This 'extenuation' would lead from a 'scene of iniquity which was without a parallel'. This iniquity done to him was authenticated by documents and was 'incredible'. He reaffirmed to the jury that the Attorney General had 'stated that he has not the slightest imputation against my honour or character up until the fatal catastrophe' – a catastrophe that must be 'long lamented' and which he regretted 'with the utmost sincerity'. He asserted no one could feel more pain on the subject than he did, with the exception of Sir Spencer Perceval's family. There is no doubt that in his disturbed mind this was indeed genuine; he believed he had been persecuted for eight years by circumstances and driven to despair. Indeed, he asserted, the British government had given him a *carte blanche* to do whatever he thought right to deal with the situation. For eight years, he had searched for justice and now 'unexpectedly' he had been called to judgment. Unexpected because he had not been given time to prepare all the documents he needed or gather the witnesses who could prove his case. He warned the jury they would have to be taken back to 1804 because that is when his 'misery' started. He was now going to go through the circumstances and read to them the petitions, letters he had written and the replies. It was these circumstances which 'unfortunately for me, Mr Perceval and for the country at large, have ended in a manner so melancholy and tragical'. What then poured forth was a powerful litany of his suffering interspersed with readings from his letters and papers. In the main he spoke firmly and with resolve, although at times his emotions would rise and he had to check them back. The story of his Russian arrests and incarceration tumbled from his lips. The pain of the humiliations and the sufferings were shared with the jury. In tears, he recounted the tragedy of his wife and her sufferings, along with those of his children. The Russian authorities had also ill-used him and had rejected his efforts to gain justice. The horrors of the Russian imprisonment were recounted. With deep emotion, he complained about Gower and Shairp and their alleged lack of assistance:

> 'My God! My God!
>   What heart could hear such excruciating tortures, without bursting with indignation at conduct so diametrically opposite to justice and to humanity? I appeal to you, gentlemen of the Jury, as men - I appeal to you as brothers - I appeal to you as Christians - whether, under such circumstances of persecution, it was possible for me to regard the actions of the Ambassador and Consul of my own country, with any other feelings but those of detestation and horror!'

Was it anger, despair or calculation that made his cry out the opening of Psalm 22 as he appealed to Christians? Furthermore, if he had met Gower it would have been him and not Perceval who would have received the pistol shot?

> 'Had I been so fortunate as to have met Lord Leveson Gower, instead of that truly amiable, and highly lamented individual, Mr. Perceval, he is the man who should have received the ball!'

The jury and the court were taken aback by this remark and a murmur ran round the courtroom. Bellingham also paused realising perhaps what he had just done. He was asked if he had any more to say.

Bellingham went through letter after letter that rejected the justice he felt he deserved. He painted a picture of a cold authority that had not understood or accepted his right for the justice that he felt was due to him. He spoke of Perceval's rejection of his request to place the petition before parliament. The deepness of his disappointment had marked him:

> 'Such gentlemen, continued to be my forlorn condition. My prayers were rejected whenever offered. I saw myself reduced to utter ruin. I was involved in debt without any possible means of extrication. I was sinking under the pressure of accumulated miseries brought on, not by my own indiscretion, but by the injustice of others. The Attorney General has told you, and he has told you truly, that till this period my name, my character, were without a blemish till this melancholy, this deplorable transaction, which no man, I can solemnly assure you, laments more deeply than I do – 'till this fatal moment my life, was without reproach.'

At this he once more burst into a flood of tears and with emotion continued to address the jury:

> 'But gentlemen, place yourselves in my situation. Your wives, your children, reduced to poverty – calling on you for help which you cannot give: looking up to you for assistance which you must deny. Gentlemen! What would your feelings be, thus goaded on? What would your alternative be?'

It would be easy for the jury to get caught up in the emotional moment. However, the facts were not fully as he described. Had his character been without blemish? What about the running away from his apprenticeship, his bankruptcy and his time in the debtors' prison in Hull? How can he claim the refusal to be unable to financially support his family, when he spent so much time and money pursuing the lost cause of his claims against the government? Where is there any trace of his taking any responsibility for the situation in Russia, when he could have made an exit from St Petersburg without any further imprisonment? It would appear that he had deluded himself into actually believing that what he was saying was true. He had become convinced that the pursuit of his idea of justice was justified by the poverty and neglect of his family.

Bellingham continued his defence by referring once more to letters and meetings with officials. Ultimately, he argued, he had been told by Mr Hill, Secretary of State at the Treasury, that he must take whatever action he felt necessary. This carte blanche then allowed him to seek justice through the killing of Perceval. Having recited the facts of the case with his own interpretation of them, he now read a document he had written the previous evening. It was the summation of his defence:

> 'Gentlemen, whenever I appear before the tribunal of my God, I shall appear there as innocent of the wilful murder of Mr Perceval, as they, who, after judgment, are admitted among the angels of Heaven. That my

arm destroyed him, I allow; that he perished by my hand, I admit but to constitute felony, there must be malice prepense, there must be the wilful intention, and I deny that it has been proved. Unless proved, however, the felony cannot be made out - this you will shortly hear from the Bench, and in that case you must acquit me. Recollect, Gentlemen, what was my situation; recollect that my family was ruined, and myself destroyed, merely, because it was Mr. Perceval's pleasure that justice should not be granted sheltering himself behind the imagined security of his station, and trampling upon law and right, in the belief that no retribution could reach him.

'Of that departed gentleman I do not wish to speak with disrespect; I do not wish to say anything in disparagement of the virtues which he was allowed to possess; and when I speak of him, I speak of him only in reference to myself. In a case so strong as mine, when I demanded justice, I demanded only my right, and not a favour; I demanded What is the birth right and privilege of every Englishman. Gentlemen, when a Minister sets himself above the laws, as Mr. Perceval did, he does it at his own personal risk. If this were not so the mere will of the Minister would become the law, and what would then become of your liberties? As to any malicious intention towards Mr. Perceval, or any desire to injure him, I solemnly avow that it was most averse from my heart. Justice and justice alone, was my object. I was driven to despair, to agony and to ruin by the conduct of Ministers.

'I gave notice at Bow Street, that if my claims were finally rejected, I would do myself justice, and that solely to ascertain in a criminal Court of Justice whether a Minister of England has a right to refuse justice to a subject of the realm. I have done so and I again repeat that the direct refusal of justice on the part of the entire Administration was the sole cause of this sad catastrophe and his Majesty's Ministers have now to reflect on their own impure conduct, which has deprived the country of the talents of Mr Perceval. It is a melancholy fact that to warp justice on any pretext or under any circumstances is the cause of all moral evil. If this position needs any proof the unfortunate event which you are now assembled to decide affords that proof.

'The cruelty of my case must be obvious to you. If a poor but unfortunate man stops another upon the highway and robs him of a few shillings, he is deprived of his life but I have been robbed of thousands by the Government; I have been deprived of everything; I have been imprisoned for years; my wife, my family, have been ruined; and I am now called to answer for my life, because Mr. Perceval chose to patronise iniquity. What then must be the crime of the Government towards me? And yet it goes unpunished. Is there any comparison between the two cases! It is a mite to a mountain. I had no alternative but to sink into utter ruin, or to take the melancholy step which

I have adopted. I was prompted to it by no malice prepense I was incited by the hope of bringing into court my unfortunate case, without which I knew it never could be promulgated; and l was incited by the desire of afterwards returning to the bosom of my family with comfort and honour. I trust that this serious lesson will operate as a warning to all future Ministers and that they will henceforth do the thing that is right - for if the upper ranks of society are permitted to act wrong with impunity, the inferior ramifications will soon become wholly corrupted.

'Gentlemen, my life is in your hands. I rely confidently upon your justice. I know not what your verdict may be; but sooner than suffer what I have done for the last eight years, five hundred deaths would be preferable. If I am destined to sacrifice my life, I shall meet my doom with conscious tranquillity. I shall look forward to it as the weary traveller looks for the promised inn, where he may repose his wearied frame after enduring the pelting of the pitiless storm. Gentlemen, it will now remain between God and your consciences as to what your verdict will be. I submit to the *fiat* of my fate, firmly anticipating an acquittal from a charge so abhorrent to every feeling of my soul.'

He now slumped back into his chair agitated and weeping bitterly He asked for a glass of water, which was provided but he continued 'for some time in great perturbation of mind'. There is no doubt this was a highly charged emotional rendering of Bellingham's tribulations and mental anguish. However, it also reveals his continued refusal to see any blame in his own behaviour. It is astonishing in many ways that in this prepared and studied statement, he blames Perceval for his own assassination. It is not only justice that he now is looking for but the 'thousands' he believed the Government had robbed him of.

Bellingham's defence team found themselves at a loss as to how to proceed. They knew that it was an impossible task to obtain a not guilty verdict. However, they ploughed on calling, Anne Billet to the stand. She appeared distressed and in a state of 'horror', according to the reports. There is no doubt she had a deep affection for Bellingham, having grown up with him in those halcyon days in St Neots. She knew him better than anyone and her shock at reading the papers naming him as the assassin of the Prime Minister caused her immediate coming up to London from her Southampton home. After being sworn in, she informed the court that Bellingham had lived at Liverpool from where he came last Christmas. His wife and children still resided there and he had carried out the trade of a merchant. She recounted the sadness of the death of his father whilst insane. She offered the opinion that Bellingham had been 'deranged' for the past three years. She had not seen him for about twelve months, but she thought him deranged every time the Russian affair was mentioned. She said her and her friends avoided mentioning

Russia in his company as it proved 'a source of uneasiness from their effect on his mind'.

Sir Vicary Gibbs' assistant, William Garrow, conducted the cross examination of Anne. He was brutal in his attitude to her and like a lamb with a wolf the questions came thick and fast:

> 'Garrow: This purpose of being in London a year ago was for the purpose of pursuing the same object, what do you mean by pursuing the same object
>
> Anne: That of going to government for redress of grievances.
>
> Garrow: And to use your own words in your own opinion you considered he was in a state of perfect derangement?
>
> Anne: Yes, I do. He has been more than three years in a state of derangement, and since he has been in London he has been pursuing the same plan, and for a long time before that. When he was in Russia when he was pursuing the same object as soon as he returned home all his friends were well convinced that was the case.'

Anne was desperate to paint her cousin as mad in order to keep him from the hangman. Garrow ignored her plea for his insanity:

> 'G. I think you spoke of him as a married man?
>
> A. Yes, he has a wife – she carries on the millinery business at Liverpool.
>
> G. I suppose that he some male friends?
>
> A. Yes.
>
> G. Do you know that he was engaged as a merchant?
>
> A. Yes.
>
> G. Do you know any of the persons that he was engaged in business with?
>
> A. No.
>
> G. Do not you know the name of any one person that he was in business with at Liverpool?'

Garrow was painting his own picture of a very normal man with family and conducting business:

> 'A. No, not one. I was in the house with his family at Liverpool – I did not know anybody that he was concerned in trade with.'

Garrow was exposing her as someone who perhaps did not know him well at all, not able to name even 'one person':

> 'A: I was in the house more than a week. I would wish to mention one circumstance which strongly confirmed me in my opinion, and a strong

mark of insanity. Two years ago last Christmas he had been telling me of his great schemes that he had pursued, he said that he had realized more than an hundred thousand pounds, with which he intended to buy an estate in the west of England, and to take a house in London; I asked him where the money was, he said he had not got the money, but it was the same as if he had; for that he had gained his cause in Russia, and our government must make it good to him; this he repeatedly said to me and his wife, but neither she nor I gave any credit to it; he then told Mrs. Bellingham and myself, to convince us of the truth of it, he would take us to the secretary of state's office; he did so, and we saw Mr. Smith the secretary. When Mr. Smith came to us, he told Mr. Bellingham that if he had not known that he had ladies with him, he would not have come at all Mr. Bellingham then told him the reason he had brought us, that it was to convince us that his claim was just, and that he should very soon have the money. Mr. Bellingham said – Sir, my friends say that I am out of my senses, is it your opinion, Mr. Smith, that I am so, Mr. Smith said, it is a very delicate question for me to answer, I only know you upon this business, and I can assure you, that you will never have what you are pursuing after, or something to that effect. We then took our leave of Mr. Smith, and when we got into the coach, he took-hold of his wife's hand, and said, now I hope my dear, you are well convinced all will happen well, and as I wished, and as he had informed us, to which we felt indignant, that he should have taken us to an office, and made us appear in the light he did.

G. How long is this ago, pray ma'am?

A. This was last Christmas two years.'

Now Garrow was making clear that any insanity described by Anne was a long time ago and not related to the time of the assassination:

'G. I think you stated that he has been in town from last Christmas?

A. Yes.

G. Has he been staying in London all that time?

A. Yes.

G. Has he been pursuing the same plan?

A. I understood all along that he was here pursuing the same object at the public offices.

G. And upon that object you always considered him in a perfect state of derangement?

A. I did.

G. Mr. Smith received you with politeness and attention?

A. Yes he did.

G. How long did you remain in town after that?

A. Till the next midsummer.'

Establishing the distance in time from the murder of any insanity was important to Garrow:

'G. In the same family with the prisoner?

A. No, I saw him frequent.

G. Was he under any restraint at that time?

A. Not at that time.

G. Were you in habits of intimacy with his family?

A. Yes.

G. If he was coerced you must have known it?

A. I think I must.

G. If there had been any restraint do you think it would have happened without your knowing it?

A. I do not know that it could.

G. Where did he live when you were in London, at the time you went to the secretary's office?

A. I think Theobald's road; his wife was in town then, she was on a visit with me.

G. And he was living by himself at the time that all his friends' thought him in a state of perfect derangement?

A. Yes.

G. Can you state any period or month, or a week, or a single day, he was ever?

A. No.

G. At no period from his return from Russia?

A. Not as I know of.

G. Has he been left to act upon his own will as much as me, or of anybody else?

A. Yes. I believe he was.

G. Did you ever communicate to the government that he was in a deranged state?

A. No.

G. After your visit to Mr. Smith, at the secretary of state's office he remained in town, and after that, either you nor his wife give any intimation to Mr. Smith that he was a deranged man, or to any of the officers of government?

A. No.

G. How long is it ago since you saw him?

A. More than a twelve month ago.

G. Did it consist with your knowledge that he carried fire arms about him.

A. No.

G. Did you ever know him confined for a single day?

A. No.'

Garrow had done his job well with Anne. She could not establish any recent derangement and furthermore could not testify to any restraints on Bellingham. She had also never informed any authority of any derangement of him. Her evidence would be of no help to the defence. Alley was desperate and turned to Mary Clarke now on the stand to state her affidavit and evidence. She was treated like Anne in the cross-examination:

'Garrow: Where do you live?

Mary Clarke: No. 7, Bagnio Court, Newgate Street. I have known the prisoner since his return from Russia, I have known him several years, but I have known most of him since he returned from Russia, about two years and a half, I have been in company with him several times.

G. Can you form any judgment respecting the state of his mind ever since he came from Russia?

M. It is my opinion that he has been disordered in his mind. I have seen him six or seven times; the last time I saw him was last January; I saw him at No. 20, North-street, Red Lion-square, I did not see any particular derangement then, I had but very little conversation with him then, he said he came upon business, he might not stay above ten days or a week, I did not see him above ten minutes at that time.

G. He came up from Liverpool to London he came up alone?

M. Yes, he left his wife, and he came up alone, to the best of my knowledge, he told me that he was come on business.

G. He transacted business for himself then, did not he?

M. I did not know anything about his business.

G. You do not know anybody that transacted businesses for him do you?

M. No, I heard that he was confined in Russia.

G. For all that he was suffered to go about here in this country?

M. I do not know of any control over him.

G. Or do you know of any medical person being consulted about him?

M. No, I do not know.

G. You do not know of any precautions that were taken to prevent him from squandering his property, in this state of derangement, do you?

M. I do not.

G. You do not know of any course pursued to him by his friends that would not be pursued to any rational man?

M. I do not.'

One wonders why she was ever called by the defence. She too could not confirm any recent derangement and only confirmed him to be able to act normally as 'a rational man'. His landlady could not appear 'due to illness', despite being subpoenaed; she probably wanted to avoid the publicity. Her servant maid, Catherine Figgins, who appears to have been incorrectly named by many sources, official and unofficial, took the stand. All she could confirm was the normality of Bellingham and that she knew nothing of the pistols. She recounted her version of the events of the day before and on the day of the assassination that have already been described. Whilst the details were largely the same as the affidavit of her employer, the details of times and dates slightly differed, but to no great degree that would help Bellingham. Her evidence on Bellingham confirmed she, 'thought he was not so well as he had been for some time past' but there was no evidence of derangement or of any visits from doctors. Alley was desperate. The Old Bailey record notes:

> 'Mr. Alley, counsel for the prisoner, directed the door-keeper to call at the door for the purpose of ascertaining whether any witnesses had arrived from Liverpool; shortly after, Mr. Sheriff Heygate announced to the bench that he had been informed two persons had, within the few last minutes, arrived from Liverpool in a post chaise and four, to give evidence in favour of the prisoner, these persons being admitted into court, looked at the prisoner, but declared he was not the person they supposed him to be; they mentioned the circumstance of their having heard of the apprehension of the prisoner, and knowing something of a person bearing his description, in whose conduct they had seen frequent marks of derangement.'

Lord Chief Justice Mansfield began to sum up the case. It has to be asked if the summing up was as impartial as it should have been. His description of the victim emphasised his goodness and thus the contrasting wickedness of his killer. Whilst the legality and content of his address was otherwise correct, his behaviour and demeanour was not. The Old Bailey record again states:

> 'Gentlemen of the jury, you are now to try an indictment which charges the prisoner at the bar with the wilful murder (here the learned judge was so hurt by his feelings, that he could not proceed for several seconds) of Mr. Spencer Perceval, (in a faint voice) who was murdered with a pistol loaded with a bullet; when he mentioned the name of (here again his lordship was sincerely affected, and burst into tears, in which he was joined by the greatest portion of the persons in court) a man so dear, and so revered as that of Mr. Spencer Perceval, I find it difficult to suppress my feelings. As, however, to say anything of the distinguished talents and virtues of that excellent man, might tend to excite improper emotions in the minds of the jury, but would with-hold these feelings which pressed for utterance from my heart, and leave you, gentlemen, to form your judgment upon the evidence which has been adduced in support of the case, undressed by any unfair indignation which you might feel against his murderer, [or] by any description, however faint, of the excellent qualities of the deceased. 'Gentlemen, you are to try the unfortunate man at the bar, in the same

manner, as if he was arraigned for the murder of any other man. The law protected all his Majesty's subjects alike, and the crime was the same whether committed upon the person of the highest and most distinguished character in the country, as upon that of the lowest. The only question you have to try is, whether the prisoner did wilfully and maliciously murder Mr. Spencer Perceval or not. It is not necessary to go very minutely into the evidence which has been produced to the fact, as there is little doubt as to the main object of your enquiry. The first thing you have to say is, whether the person charged with having murdered him; and whether that murder had been committed with a pistol bullet.'

The judge then began to recount the evidence of witnesses, at one point describing Bellingham's claims as 'supposed grievances'. He then addressed the matter of Bellingham believing he was justified in his killing Perceval:

'Such dreadful reasoning could not be too strongly reprobated. If a man fancied he was right and in consequence conceived that that fancy was not gratified, he had a right to obtain justice by any means which his physical strength gave him, there is no knowing where so pernicious a doctrine might end. If a man fancies he has a right, and endeavours to assert that right, is he to put to death the persons who refuses to give him any reparation to that which he supposes himself entitled. By the same reason every person who presided in a court of judicature refusing to give to a suitor in an action, what he requires, would be liable to revenge equally atrocious.'

The implication of these comments was obvious; Bellingham could not rely on this 'pernicious' doctrine. The learned judge then turned to the issue of insanity that was proposed as a defence. He outlined the ways a person could be deemed to be insane under the law of the land and then advised the jury:

'The witnesses who had been called to support this extraordinary defence, had given a very singular account, to shew that at the, commission of the crime the prisoner was insane. What might have been the state of his mind some time ago was perfectly immaterial. The single question is, whether at the time this fact was committed, he possessed a sufficient degree of understanding to distinguish good from evil, right from wrong, and whether murder was a crime not only against the law of God, but against the law of his country. Here it appears that the prisoner had gone out like another man; that he came up to London by himself, at Christmas last, that he was under no restraint, that no medical man had attended him to cure his malady, that he was perfectly regular in all his habits, in short there was no proof adduced to shew that his understanding was so deranged, as not to enable him to know that murder was a crime. On the contrary, the testimony adduced in his defence, has most distinctly proved, from a description of his general demeanour, that he was in every respect a full and competent judge of all his actions.

'Having then commented on the evidence of Mrs. Clarke, Mrs. Billet, and Mary Figgins, his Lordship concluded by advising the jury to take all the facts into their most serious consideration. If you have any doubt, you will give the prisoner the benefit of that doubt; but if you conceive him guilty of the crime alleged against him, in that case you will find him guilty.'

Here again the judge was very sure that Bellingham was not insane at the time of the assassination. Indeed, that was the frequent response of the newspapers. The editor of *Bell's Weekly Chronicle* sums up the general feeling of most observers:

'The truth seems therefore to be, that it was the act of a most wicked and malignant nature working itself up to its highest possible pitch and, in the language of the criminal himself, maturing and familiarising a most horrible purpose to the mind by frequent and intense meditation, and gradually formed resolution. The ultimate result therefore might possibly have the character of madness, in the same manner as the act of a drunken man, might be immediately imputed to his intoxication, but as the madness and the intoxication were the works of a preceding will, they are therefore full imputable and the objects of human punishment.'

However, the final decision would be the jury's and to them the matter was handed over. After about three minutes of discussion in the jury box, they asked to be allowed to retire for further consideration. Fifteen minutes later they returned with their verdict: GUILTY.

There could have been no expectation from the defence, except Bellingham himself, of anything else. He had whispered to his attorney as the jury filed out that a note should be sent to his wife, by the evening post, telling her he was free. So it was a very disappointed man who was asked if he wished to say anything on the verdict and, as he indicated not, the judge addressed him:

'Prisoner at the bar! you have been convicted by a most attentive and a most merciful jury, of one of the most malicious and atrocious crimes it is in the power of human nature to perpetrate - that of wilful and premeditated murder! A crime which in all ages and in all nations has been held in the deepest detestation - a: crime as odious and abominable in the eyes of God, as it is hateful and abhorrent to the feelings of man - A crime which, although thus heinous in itself, in your case has been heightened by every possible feature of aggravation. You have shed the blood of a man admired for every virtue which can adorn public or private life - a man, whose suavity and meekness of manner was calculated to disarm all political rancour, and to deprive violence of its asperity. By his death, charity has lost one of its greatest promoters; religion, one of its firmest supporters; domestic society, one of its happiest and sweetest examples; and the country, one of its brightest ornaments - a man, whose ability and worth was likely to produce lasting advantages to this empire, and ultimate benefit to the world. Your crime has this additional feature of atrocious guilt, that in the midst of civil society, unarmed, defenceless, in the fulfilment of his public duty, and within the very verge of the sanctuary of the law, your impure hand has deprived of existence a man as universally beloved, as preeminent for his talents and excellence of heart. To indulge in any conjecture as to the motive which could have led you to the commission of this atrocious deeds, would be to enquire into all that is base and perfidious in the human heart. - Assassination is most horrid and revolting to the soul of man, inasmuch as it is calculated to render bravery useless and cowardice successful. It is therefore that the voice of God himself has declared, "that he that sheddeth man's blood, by man shall his blood be shed." In conformity to these laws, which God hath ordained, and men have obeyed your disgraced and indignant country, by the example of your ignominious fate, will appreciate the horror of your offence, and set up a warning to all others who might hereafter be tempted to the perpetration of a crime of so deep a dye. A short time, a very short time, remains for you to supplicate for that mercy in another world, which public justice forbids you to expect in this. Sincerely do I hope that the short interval that; has elapsed since the commission of this atrocious offence has not been unemployed by you in soliciting that pardon from the Almighty which I trust your prayers may obtain, through the merits of your Redeemer, whose first attribute is mercy. It only now remains for me to pass the dreadful sentence of the law, which is – That you be taken from hence to the place from whence you came, and from thence to a place of execution, where you shall be hanged by the neck until you be dead; your body to be dissected and anatomized.'

It was reported that the Judge's delivery was 'unusually excellent and so powerful was its effect on us all'. The listeners to this speech were as a body moved to tears.

Bellingham appeared to want to speak with a faint 'My Lord ...' being heard but he was silenced by Newman, his jailer, and told that this was not the appropriate time to say anything. Some reports said he was 'most affected' whilst others reported Bellingham showed no emotion at the verdict, seemingly believing he had said all there was to say as to the character of Perceval. With a slight stumble on the sloping floor of the courtroom he was escorted from the court and returned to Newgate prison to await his execution. At Newgate, he was not returned to the cell he had previously occupied but to the condemned prisoner's cell. It was

Middlefex Prifoners upon Orders.

1 *James Goff,*
2 *Mary Beft,*
3 *Eleanor* alias *Ellen Chambers,*

Executed.

attainted May Seffion, 1812, of ftealing in a dwelling-houfe and forgery, and feverally received judgment of death.

4 *John Bellingham,* attainted May Seffion, 1812, of the wilful murder of the Right Hon. Spencer Perceval, and ordered to be hanged by the neck until he be dead, and his body delivered over to the Surgeons to be diffected and anatomized, purfuant to the ftatute, &c.

5 *George Hammon,* attainted Feb. Seffion, 1812, of felony, but an objection in point of Law arifing, and the Court not being advifed, his judgment was refpited, and he was in May Seffion, 1812, ordered and adjudged to be

Bellingham's judgement record.

a narrow cell of six feet by nine feet, with a nine-foot-high ceiling. The door was made of four inch thick wood. In this confined space, Bellingham would have the company of two prison officers to watch for suicide attempts and to monitor visitors to the cell. However, Bellingham was completely composed with no signs of any emotional disturbance. His conversation was polite and appreciative of the assistance from his jailers. He asked for some tea but was informed that until the execution he was only able to be given bread and water. This was a situation he was used to in Russia and he accepted it without complaint. He drank liberally from a pitcher of water supplied to him and ate a large amount of the bread. His only allusion to the forthcoming execution was to express that 'he would be happy to be out of existence'. In our portrait of this assassin, the remark gives insight into his mind. It reveals a man who has been through a life of disappointment. He had lost his father and fell on the good offices of others for his progress in life. Yet he had himself spurned these good people and ran from their attempts to set him up in a good position for his future. He had struggled to become a competent businessman, with bankruptcy, debtors' prison and the horrors of Russia that had brought him to great depths of woe. A burning passion within him had created a deluded and truly held belief of a need for justice that would restore his reputation and a wealth he had never had. In England, the flame of that passion was slowly killed by the cold water of reality that was poured on it by the government and its ministers. The expected verdict of justification and release had not been given and now the noose of the executioner beckoned. Bellingham had no more fight left in him and looked to death for the freedom for which he longed. Yet there is no doubt that within the man there was a great conflict, which he controlled in his outer expression. As he slept that night, unrestrained by the conscious, his watchers recorded some 'violent' contortions as if he was in the midst of a bad dream. Their observations point once more to the unconscious of Bellingham. Here, unguarded by consciousness, he would have been wrestling with the reality of his life, the delusional state of his beliefs and the impending certainty of death. His bodily contortions reflected his mental contortions that struggled for reconciliation.

His disturbed sleep meant that he awoke at a much later time than usual. Around ten fifteen he was given bread and water, being denied the tea he would have preferred. He was also refused some 'jelly' that he had asked for as he was feeling faint. The claustrophobia of the cell was relieved by Newman keeping the cell door open and allowing him to walk between rooms. For this he expressed his heartfelt gratitude. He handed his Bible to one of his keepers and asked that a passage be read to him, chapters four and five of the First Epistle of St John. These chapters would remind him of the call to love one another. No doubt as he faced his death, the words of the Apostle would be seen by Bellingham as comfort:

> 'In this is love brought to perfection among us, that we have confidence on the Day of Judgment because as he is, so are we in this world. There is no fear in love, but perfect love drives out fear because fear has to do with punishment, and so one who fears is not yet perfect in love.'

Despite appearing to show no sorrow or repentance for his act, Bellingham still spoke in Christian terms. He seemed 'perfectly composed' and 'resigned to his fate' and declared that 'he would soon be with his Heavenly Father and released from all his trouble'. Dr Ford, the Prison Chaplain, took the matter up with him when he visited him for an hour. He exhorted him to ask for forgiveness and 'fervently prayed for him'. Later that night, Newman and Davis, the head keepers, visited him and asked after his health. He said he 'was very well and would soon be out of his troubles'. At eleven o'clock, Newman returned with Mr Butterworth, 'a respected bookseller of Fleet Street'. Bellingham was glad to see him and the two men spent some time in 'religious conversation' in which they argued 'zealously' about three Scripture references that Bellingham was using to justify his action. He argued that in a 'few hours more he would be in a better country'. Butterworth also wanted to clarify two points: 'Was there another person or persons involved?' and 'Where did he obtain the pistols?' To the first Bellingham replied, 'No! I do solemnly swear there was not.' He also confirmed the purchase of the pistols from Beckwith's shop. When Butterworth was leaving, Bellingham informed him that he would be writing a letter to his wife. It was therefore in the early hours of Sunday morning he was given pen and paper. He sat down and wrote his last thoughts for Mary:

> 'My Blessed Mary,
>
> 'It rejoiced me beyond measure to hear you are likely to be well provided for. I am sure the public at large will participate in, and mitigate, your sorrows; I assure you, my love, my sincerest endeavours have ever been directed to your welfare. As we shall not meet any more in this world,

I sincerely hope we shall do so in the world to come. My blessing to the boys, with kind remembrance to Miss Stevens, for whom I have the greatest regard, in consequence of her uniform affection for them. With the purest intentions, it has always been my misfortune to be thwarted, misrepresented, and ill-used in life; but, however, we fuel a happy prospect of compensation in a speedy translation to life eternal. It's not possible to be more calm or placid than I feel, and nine hours more will waft me to those happy shores where bliss is without alloy.

Your ever affectionate,
John Bellingham'

This letter gives particular insight into Bellingham's character in what is left out. This man is writing to a woman who has borne him children in the greatest of difficulty both in Russia and in England. She has endured hardship and penury, having to turn to a trade to earn money, whilst he squandered the family income on a fantasy. There are no words of appreciation or thanks – no remembrances of their married life together – no words of intimacy for her as a lover or woman. Rather there is a 'rejoicing' that the public will do what he should have done. Indeed, Miss Stevens too, is remembered for her role in making up for his fatherly absences. Once more his refrain is that it was not his fault. He had 'the purest intentions', but he was 'ill-used'; even at the end there is no acknowledgement of personal responsibility. He had avoided that all his life. These things must have on his conscience, as he later added a PS:

'Dr Ford will forward you my watch, my prayer book with a guinea and note. Once more, God be with you, my sweet Mary. The public sympathise much for me, but I have been called upon to play an anxious card in life.'

Whilst there is the 'sweet Mary' the focus ends on himself and his own 'anxious card'. As he returned to his bed, his mind must have been still turning over the letter and its contents. He felt the need to explain why he had lost his case. It of course was not due to a failure on his part and his denial of what he felt was justice; he needed someone to blame. He later added a note to the letter, reported in the press that again made others responsible:

'That the unfortunate man was afflicted with a strange malady, which occasionally rendered him incapable of correct conclusions, must be evident from the following note, which he wrote the night preceding his execution: "I lost my suit solely through the improper conduct of my attorney and counsel, Mr. Alley, in not bringing my witnesses forward (of whom there were more than twenty): in consequence, the judge took advantage of the circumstance, and I went off [on] the defence without having brought forward a single friend – otherwise I must inevitably have been acquitted".'

This was more delusion. Alley had done his best with the lot he had received. He had to work within time frames set by the court. He had made attempts to get people to testify and had managed to get Anne Billet and Mary Clarke to the stand. He had Catherine the maid to confirm Bellingham's good 'character' and had made some attempt to get a claim of insanity accepted. It was Bellingham himself who destroyed that line of defence. The 'inevitability' of acquittal was never a realistic possibility. Bellingham ate some bread and then lay back to sleep.

Sunday saw him visited by Alderman Matthew Wood, who, on enquiring how he was, was told by Bellingham, 'As well as a man can be subsisting upon bread and water!' He went on to defiantly declare:

'Government think to intimidate me, but they are mistaken, I have been guilty of no offence, having only done an act of public justice.'

He was attended to by the prison Ordinary, who attended to his spiritual needs. The *Leeds Mercury* reporter noted:

'He appeared rather dejected, but dwelt on the promises of the Gospel, and hopes of a blessed immortality, through the mediation of the Redeemer. He was particular in his inquiries as to the hour and place of execution, and remarked that – "Life had been a weary pilgrimage to him – the bliss fleeting and illusory – the misery permanent and real; in laying down, he had no vain regrets to make." In this strain he continued the conversations for some time, but could not be brought to make any acknowledgement of the heinousness of the crime he had committed'

The day was filled with such visits of sincere men caring for Bellingham's soul but all failing to obtain any confession of guilt or regret for his actions. One particular Minister of Religion, Daniel Wilson, had a prolonged visit and conversation, which was published after Bellingham's death. This is of importance as it was designed 'to throw light on so dreadful a character'.

Wilson found Bellingham reclining on his bed when he entered the cell. He rose from the bed and greeted the minister and another friend with 'civility'. He was informed of the purpose of the visit which was for his real benefit and for the concern the good man had for Bellingham's state and his meeting with God. Bellingham was asked if that would be acceptable, to which he replied, 'Undoubtedly. No topic can be more interesting to me.' With this, Wilson decided to move carefully forward, avoiding any mention of the assassination at the beginning. Rather, he outlined the theological understanding of the Christian faith, through the holiness of God and the sinfulness of man. He gently moved to suggest to Bellingham that in the abhorrence of sin by God, a man was to be repentant of his sin. He paused for silence, in the expectation that Bellingham might admit his full guilt of the crime. However, there was no such admission, Bellingham simply agreeing that 'I know myself to be a sinner; we come into the world sinners'. Wilson was disappointed and noted the insincerity of the response. Wilson once more embarked on an explanation of love, grace and sincere repentance and the need for acknowledgement of transgression. Despite heartfelt delivery and the quoting of Scripture, it fell on stony ground. Bellingham insisted he had sorted his eternal future out, insisting he had confessed his sins. However, Wilson felt this was a 'cold' acknowledgement without any real sorrow. His friend then took up the plea to Bellingham asking if he felt that deep sorrow and a hungering after salvation. Bellingham disappointed him by stating he could not feel anything of this.

Wilson tried again to bring home his desire for Bellingham to repent and gave more encouragements of the Christian faith. Suddenly he stopped and told Bellingham that he was not showing any real sense of sorrow or desire for salvation and asked that he allow him to pray for the Holy Spirit to melt his heart. Bellingham civilly agreed and allowed the good man to call upon his God to that affect. Despite the man's sincere passion when he had finished, Bellingham's response shocked him. He wrote, 'I am sure every reader will shudder, when I relate the prisoner replied to all this, with perfect apathy, "True Sir. None of us know what will take place after death".' Despite all Bellingham's protestations of a happier place and meeting God, this indeed was a strange response. The shocked Wilson retorted, 'Nobody Knows!' and went on to recount Scriptures and urged reconsideration by Bellingham. He was blunt in declaring to Bellingham that he was damned if he did not repent. He now believed that, despite all Bellingham's saying he believed in Scripture, he in fact was 'under the influence of an evil heart of unbelief'.

Bellingham's calm and tranquil manner throughout all this caused him to have a 'dejected' mind and he did not know how to proceed. His friend then produced a letter. Before reading it, he suggested to Bellingham that Perceval may never have personally seen his papers. Bellingham was dismissive of such an idea, 'O, he must have known!'. The letter was from Perceval to a Mr Dickinson, a humble journeyman printer. He had found himself in difficulties with a sick wife and three children to care for. He had written to Perceval for help. Perceval responded by giving a gift of £11 2s 6d (£735). On reading the letter, Bellingham responded 'in a chilling tone', 'This was very kind to be sure!'. He remained unmoved to any sense of regret or sorrow for his deed. Wilson continued to be more direct against the hardened attitude of Bellingham. He read another letter, this time about Perceval's wife who it was reported had prayed for her husband's murderer. Bellingham, who had been staring steadfastly at his visitors, dropped his head and appeared affected by the letter, but within moments had regained himself and coldly stated, 'This was a Christian spirit! She must be a good woman. Her conduct was more like a Christian's than my own, certainly.'

The laudable Minister was horrified by Bellingham's demeanour. He decided to directly challenge him:

> '"Can that justify you in taking what you are pleased to call justice into your own hands; and, on your own private opinion, without inquiry, without trial, without judge or jury, without one form of law, to hurry a fellow-creature, one who never offered you any offence, without a moment's time for reflection or prayer, into eternity, by the treacherous blow of an assassin? For Mr. Perceval," I added, "died, I believe, almost immediately."'

Here was the nub of the matter. Wilson believed he had stripped away any excuse of insanity and any attempt to claim he acted in the name of justice. The response chilled him:

> '"Yes," he answered, with an apathy which chilled my frame, as if he were giving me a species of information in which he had no especial concern; "he lived but a few minutes."'

Wilson continued to bring home to him his callous attitude and desperate spiritual situation, but Bellingham only responded that he was refused justice. The good minister soldiered on becoming even tougher in his approach:

> 'I had now almost despaired of producing any impression, but I still went on. "Can your opinion of justice being refused you, warrant your becoming the judge and executioner in your own cause? Was your view of your own case to be considered as infallible? Or, supposing your opinion correct, still can any provocation whatever palliate the foulest and most dreadful of all social enormities, the taking away the life of another? Would you have justified anyone who, on the pretence of an affront, should have dared to have planted a dagger in the bosom of your wife or child? Or, supposing you had yourself been in Mr. Perceval's situation, the prime minister of the realm, with all the private and public virtues of that excellent statesman ; supposing further, what must be the case with every minister, that you were surrounded with petitioners, whose cases it was absolutely impossible for you fully to investigate, and who were all equally positive in their claims; and that, in addition to this, you had of course all the weighty concerns of the empire pressing upon you; I ask, what should you have thought of a petitioner, merely because he had been disappointed in his application,

imagining himself a private individual, justified in assassinating you, the chief minister of the crown, incapable of intending him the smallest evil, and, at the very worst, only mistaken in your judgment, whilst in every other act of your life you were exemplary and benevolent?"'

Whether the words of Wilson on Perceval or the mention of Bellingham's wife and children, had an effect, we do not know, but this brought tears to Bellingham's eyes. The minister felt the words had hit home and Bellingham had realised what he had done, but still his words did not match his tears. After some silence and more words from the vicar, there was no change in Bellingham's position; 'I have confessed my sins before God and trust in a general amnesty of them'. Wilson, though appalled by the refusal to specifically take responsibility for the murder of Perceval, again tried using Scripture to bring Bellingham to account.

Bellingham was unmoved and only reflected on the sorrow of Perceval's widow and family. Once more Wilson was astute in his observations:

> "'It seems to me," I answered, "that you have been allowing your mind to brood over your imagined injuries so long, that you have really quite blinded your judgment, and hardened your heart, and at length brought yourself to trample on all the checks of conscience, the plainest duties of morality, the first precepts of religion, and the most positive laws of your country. And thus, instead of submitting to your difficulties with patience, as inflicted by the providence of God, and confining yourself to lawful and peaceable means for your relief, you have, by degrees, brought yourself first to commit, and then to justify, this horrible deed."'

Wilson had to leave but his friend continued in his noble cause. Still Bellingham was unmoved. As the talk turned to his childhood and his parents, he was moved to tears at the mention of his mother; however, in every other way Bellingham had been untouched by the long time spent with Wilson and his friend. Wilson recorded some details of Bellingham's history but concluded, 'The diabolical project being once deliberately formed, he seems to have proceeded to its execution with a degree of calmness and obduracy to which I know of no parallel'. What the two well-intentioned men lacked was an understanding of the mental condition under which Bellingham was held. Their approach could have never penetrated his delusional world. So it was with this attempt to bring Bellingham to accept his full responsibility for the assassination and death failing, he retired to bed. Tomorrow he had his appointment with his own death.

Chapter 14

I Am Perfectly Ready...

Monday 18 May 1812 was a day of heavy clouds that spilled their rain onto the streets of London. Arising around six o'clock, Bellingham took a shilling and handed it to Mr Walker, one of his keepers, and thanked him for his kindness. He washed and dressed himself with those around him noting his calm composure. At some point in the morning, he was again visited by Mr Butterworth, the bookseller. He spent a half of an hour reading his prayer book and was then joined by Dr Ford, the Ordinary, and they retired to a room set aside for the condemned prisoner. There he again expressed his often-stated condition, as calm, composed and ready to meet his fate with resignation. He and his minister prayed together fervently and he partook in the sacrament of communion. It was noted that he was 'deeply impressed with the truths of the Christian religion' and was caught up in 'pious religious ejaculations'. After further prayers, they were informed that the Sheriffs were ready. Bellingham replied, 'I am perfectly ready also'. They walked into the Press Yard of the gaol, where Bellingham was to have the heavy iron fetters removed. He glanced to the sky, saying, 'Ah. It rains heavily.' The removal of the fetters was a little painful causing him to cry, 'Mind, Mind. Take care, Take Care!' The man doing the job was having difficulty and Bellingham advised him, 'Strike it in the centre and more firmly and you will accomplish it.'

He looked around and looked steadily at the company gathered with 'something like a dignified air' according to the reporter from the *Hampshire Chronicle*. He noted:

> 'His face possessed the same character and colour as on Friday, during trial
> – No emotions of fear or compunction were visible. His dress was not so
> neat; on this awful occasion he wore a coat which very much resembled that
> produced in court as the one in which he assassinated Mr Perceval.'

As we continue to try and understand Bellingham in this portrait, as he stands on the edge of eternity, let us consider this conversation he had with Sheriffs Birch and Heygate. Birch asked in a very respectful manner, 'The public mind, Mr Bellingham, requires to be satisfied upon a most important point, whether any other person was in any degree connected with you in this dreadful deed, and whether it was perpetuated on any public ground?' Bellingham replied in a firm tone, 'Certainly not!' Heygate then continued the questioning; 'Then it was your own affair – it was from personal resentment?'

This appeared to hurt and upset Bellingham, who replied in a dignified tone, 'Personal Resentment? I bore no resentment to Mr. Perceval as a man – and as a man I am sorry for his fate. I was referred from Minister to Minister, from office to office, and at length refused redress for my grievances. It was my own sufferings that caused the melancholy event and I hope it will be a warning to future Ministers, to attend to the applications and prayers of those who suffer oppression. Had my Petition been brought into Parliament this catastrophe would not have happened – I am sorry for the sufferings I have caused to Mr. Perceval's family and friends'

'It would be right they should know you feel so much regret'

'You may communicate it. I wish them to know it'

'I hope you feel deep contrition for the deed?'

Bellingham, it was noted, assumed 'an air of considerable dignity'.

'I hope, Sir, I feel as a man ought to do'

'You know, that to take away the life of a man unlawfully is a heinous crime?'

'The Scriptures, you know, Sir, Say that'

'I hope you have made your peace with God and that by your repentance, you will meet the Almighty with a pure soul?'

'No one can presume to do that, Sir. No mortal can be pure in his sight, only our Saviour went from this world into His presence with a pure spirit' With this he appeared anxious to stop the questioning and with a firm but mild tone said, 'Gentlemen. I am quite ready'. Dr Ford pointed out that there was still ten minutes more. However, the executioner, William Brunskill, began the process of tying his hands and pinioning his arms. Bellingham cautioned him to 'do everything properly that I do not suffer unnecessarily'. He assured him he would. When Brunskill had finished, Bellingham asked for the ropes to be tightened more, as he did not 'wish to have the power of offering any resistance'.

Bellingham was minutes from death, yet he appeared calm and in a very rational state of mind. There was still no sense with him that what he had done is unjustified. He still maintained the belief that he acted justly, in the assassination of Perceval. There is a paradox that runs through his last days and minutes. There is the quite clear religious opinion, accepted by Bellingham, that murder is a crime against God and man. Yet he remained convinced that for him it will be excused in the hereafter. He appeared emotionally detached from his situation. Without considering a full psychological profile of Bellingham the assassin, impossible without a prolonged personal examination, we can however see in him many traits of the Detached Personality affected by persecutory delusions. From all we know of him, through his writings and life history, he appears to have had few friends, male or female. There is little evidence of communicating deep emotions, except on those occasions when faced with the Russian experiences, and then he was unable to control his tight hold on them.

Detached Personalities usually have a history of being emotionally hurt early in life, usually by those closest to them. In Bellingham's case, his most formative years were with an insane father who subsequently died when he was very young. There then followed a life of painful and difficult experiences. The response to this is to find some relief from this pain. This is often simply to just stop caring about relationships and to disconnect from close involvements. For such people, intimate relationships represent great danger, because they had not found love and safety in the most important significant relationship of all – for Bellingham, that was his father. This led to him feeling helplessness in a hostile world. Recall what he had written:

> 'I am one who never possessed the advantage of many, in having a father before me and being destitute of a friend to give me a start in life; was obliged at a tender age and uneducated, to launch unprotected, into the world, and coped with severe difficulties and unexampled severities, of which I was but too sensible'.

Whilst it could be argued that this statement denies the presence of a mother and others, it is likely that Bellingham felt detached from them, and may explain the absence from his mother's funeral – and the associated emotions. This would explain his detached approach to his death, He had said 'a few hours more he would be in a better country'. Bellingham wanted to die and to be released from his emotional prison – he had suffered enough. None of this excused him from his actions and he remained fully responsible for the murder of Perceval. Nor does it necessarily make him insane, but in a more enlightened time, greater consideration would have enquired more thoroughly into his mental state.

Everything was now ready and Brunskill respectfully reached to adjust Bellingham's cravat for easy removal on the scaffold. Bellingham sensed his carefulness and told him, 'Certainly do so. It is perfectly all right'. It was just before the execution party were about to move off, that Bellingham seemed to sense a tear forming and bowed his head to wipe it away. His tight control of his emotions was under great strain despite the outward appearance. The group moved quickly with dignity as Bellingham, described as 'more composed' than those around him, walked beside Dr Ford. The newspapers reported in agreement:

> 'He ascended the scaffold with rather a light step, a cheerful countenance, and a confident, a calm, but not at all an exulting air; he looked about him a little lightly and rapidly, which seems to have been his usual manner and gesture; but he had no air of triumph, nor disposition to pay attention to

the mob, nor did he attempt to address the populace. He submitted quietly, and with a disposition to accommodate, in having the rope fastened round his neck, nor did he seem to notice anything whatever that passed in the mob, nor was he in any way gratified by the friendly disposition which some manifested towards him.'

Dr Ford stood beside him and asked for his final words. He began to speak of Russia again but Dr Ford interrupted him and reminded him that he was about to enter eternity. They both then prayed silently together. Ford then asked how he felt and was told that he 'thanked God for having enabled him to meet his fate with so much fortitude and resignation'. Brunskill then began to put the face covering over Bellingham's head but Bellingham asked that it not be done. He was informed that it was necessary and so permitted it. Silence fell over the watching crowd and the public clock struck the hour of eight. Upon the seventh chime, the executioner released the trapdoor and Bellingham fell into eternity.

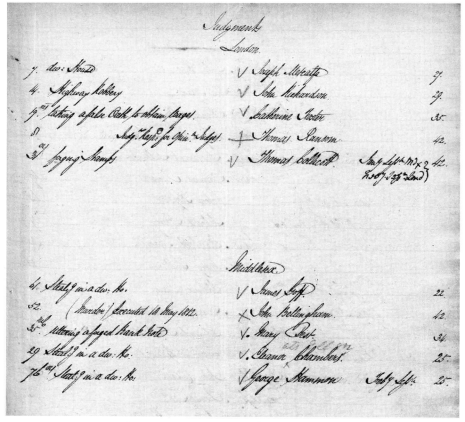

The handwritten entry in the court files recording the execution having been carried out.

Chapter 15

It Was From Personal Resentment – Or Was It?

This question of conspiracy was put to him on a number of occasions and consistently he denied anyone else was involved. He had insisted:

'… it is a private injury – I know what I have done. It was a denial of justice on the part of Government'

A question was raised at the time and indeed is still asked; was there a conspiracy which Bellingham was a part off, or did he act alone? Conspiracies were suspected everywhere and the Home Office files of the period contain warrants issued for the arrests of groups of men. One such document, of many, in 1812, lists twenty-one names and continues:

'… have been concerned in treasonable practices against his Majesty's person and Government and that they, or some of them, have entered into a correspondence with certain persons now resident in France for the purpose of carrying the object of their said treasonable conspiracies and practices into effect.'

It was therefore immediately thought that Bellingham was part of similar groups. On 13 May 1812, William Astell wrote to Ryder, at the secretary of State's office, enclosing a letter from George Cayley a 'physician of eminence'. He was 'all in a tremor' and asked that his name be kept secret. The letter contained information he had obtained that the 'nobility' would all be destroyed by 1 Jan 1813. Cayley's tremors were affecting many in high places. On 28 March 1812, Ryder was also given an anonymous letter informing him that '6,000 men' were going to visit Parliament and blow it up. The writer stated that 'labrin people cant stand it no longer'. On the very day of the assassination, Ryder received a note signed 'Death or Liberty', in which the threat of murder was made against the government, naming Lord Castlereagh in particular. A letter from Bristol immediately after the shooting informed the Prince Regent that the writer was 'settling his affairs and writing his will' and in three weeks he would 'follow the example of the illustrious Bellingham, whom God grant is in heaven now' and come up to shoot him. On 23 May 1812, an unnamed fellow Liverpudlian, signing himself 'a sufferer', wrote

BELKNAP Hon. Abraham, at Johnston, in 92d
    year ; many years member of General As-
    sembly and 44 years a Justice of the Peace.
    Gazette of   Feb. 7, 1820
    Abraham, Esq., at Johnston, in 55th year,   March 15, 1820
    Mrs. Patience, wife of Elisha, in this town,
    in 28th year,   March 11, 1823
    William, infant son of Elisha, in this town,
    aged 4 months,   March 26, 1823
BELL Robert, at Richmond, Va., in 53d year,
    printer and bookseller, for many years at
    Philadelphia,   Sept. 23, 1784
    · Mrs. Margaret, wife of William, merchant,
    and only daughter of Boston Brayton, of
    Smithfield, at Lansingburg, N. Y., in 36th
    year, (we think this word "Boston" should
    have been "Baulston." J. N. A.). Gazette
    of   Feb. 20, 1796
    Charles, at Newport, at an advanced age.
    Gazette of   March 7, 1801
    Jacob W., drowned on the Orleans beach, of
    the schooner Farmer. Gazette of   Jan. 14, 1804
    John, Esq., bookseller, at Edinburgh, Scot-
    land. Gazette of   Dec. 20, 1806
    Mrs. Mary Ann, at Calcutta, India,   Dec. 30, 1809
    Mr. ——, house carpenter, drowned in at-
    tempting to rescue a person who had fallen
    into the river, near Bloomingdale, N. Y.
    Gazette of   Sept. 7, 1816
    Shubael, Esq., at Boston, aged 53 years ; dep-
    uty sheriff and keeper of the prison there,   May 30, 1819
    William, mason, at Boston, aged 70 years.
    Gazette of   March 22, 1823
    Major John, U. S. Army, aged 40 years, at
    Henrietta, N. Y. ; was with Major Long in
    his tour across the Rocky Mountains and
    Gen. Jackson in Florida. Gazette of   May 4, 1825
BELLINGHAM John, the murderer of the
    British prime minister, executed at London,   May 18, 1812
BELLOWS Hezekiah, in 37th year,   Sept. 14, 1819
    Dr. Eleazer, Jun., in this town, aged about
    40 years,   Jan. 29, 1821
BELT William B., an officer of the bank at
    Georgetown, at Barbadoes ; his servant
    died next day.   Nov. 10, 1810
BELZONI Mr. G., the celebrated traveler, at
    Gato, Africa. Gazette of   June 5, 1824
BENBRIDGE Richard M., aged 16 years ; mid-
    shipman on board U. S. ship Peacock ;
    grandson of Com. Truxton, at Key West,   Sept. 13, 1823

The Providence Gazette death entry for Bellingham.

to the Secretary of State. He declared that 'the removal of the Premier by the Patriot Bellingham' had given hopes to thousands. In a long letter, he called him to remember the 'fortitude of Bellingham' and warned of murder if things did not change. Another communication was a statement on oath which named a number of men who had been overheard in a Public House in Cheshire, supporting the killing of Perceval and complimenting Bellingham. They also offered to raise money for his widow. A 'True Patriot' wrote of the 'joy of the event' (the assassination) and that 'many others' stood by to act. The Home Office files have a great number of similar communications and sworn affidavits of overheard conversations, which make Bellingham a patriot, courageous, martyr, a great Briton and even poems to his 'excellent' deed.

The Reverend Blacow of St Mark's Church, which was situated in Duke Street, Liverpool, where Bellingham had his home, wrote to Ryder a very concerned letter. After preaching on the goodness of Mr Perceval and condemning his death, he had received a threating letter. The writer signed himself Julius Lt. De Luddite. In it, he condemned the good man's preaching and told him if it had not been a church they were in, he would have shot him with his pistol. He went on to threaten 'sacrifices in the manner of the Brave and Patriotic Bellingham'. Indeed, it was suspected that Bellingham may have been connected to Sir Francis Burdett, after a rioter celebrating the assassination was found with a note in his pocket supporting Bellingham. Throughout England, Militia and Troops were put on alert. Until the question of conspiracy was settled, the government would take no chances.

Andro Linklater in his book, *Why Spencer Perceval Had to Die*, gives a wide and scholarly background to the times of the assassination. He paints an excellent backdrop to the many factions and concerns who all wanted to be rid of Perceval. As we have seen there were the British and American traders along with the slave traders, all being hit hard in their pockets. We then have the French and their spies in England who wanted an end to a damaging war and they in turn had sympathy from a faction worried about the drain on the Exchequer by the war. The Home Office files from 1800 to 1812 contain hundreds of reports from Militia Generals, Magistrates, Agents and others, all with the details of concern about the riots against manufacturers and the Governments attitudes to wages. Indeed, the reports of the murder of business owners were

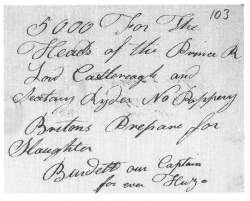

A note found in a rioter's pocket.

General Isaac Gascoyne by James Lonsdale (1777–1839). National Museums Liverpool.

common. On top of this the Poor Laws were rendering thousands destitute. From all these factions, there were conspiring groups of mainly men. Any one of them would be delighted to have had Bellingham in their midst – a man with a cause and a determination to execute his own justice to the limit. Furthermore, within the Parliamentary establishment there were also interested parties who opposed Perceval with a passion. They counted among their number military men who would have no problem using violence to solve an issue. They too would have liked to use Bellingham. General Gascoyne, for example, had said:

> 'that, in case of an invasion, besides the force of the country already on foot, the moment that real danger should approach our shore, or a foreign foe set foot upon this island, there was not a man, within or without these walls, that would not fly to arms, scorning to avail himself of any plea or exemption from the defence of his country.'

He was indeed a patriot who had stood foursquare in defending the nation against any threat and he was strongly opposed to the abolition of the slave trade. There is no suggestion he was involved in any way with Bellingham in a conspiracy but could he have done more to deflect him from his path? It is therefore easy to grasp why the government was concerned that Bellingham may not have acted alone.

In Linklater's book, he takes time to discuss the £20 promissory note from a Mr Wilson, found with Mrs Robarts. The speculation is made that it was in connection to Bellingham carrying out the assassination and that American traders were involved. However, a letter in the Home Office files dated 18 May 1812, the day Bellingham was hanged, from Butterworth, the Fleet Street bookseller, explains the £20. In the letter, to Richard Ryder, he gives a background for writing to him. He was concerned of reports from his friends in the north of England who were suffering from riots and damage to property following the assassination. He believed that he could help the situation by making certain facts known. These facts he had gained during his visits to Bellingham. He wrote:

> 'I conceive that my visits may at last answer some useful purpose by obtaining from him a solemn confirmation of his former statements, that he was engaged in no sort of conspiracy and that it was not from any kind of political motive whatever that he was induced to commit the horrid deed, but from a full infatuation of imaginary personal wrongs.'

Butterworth assured Ryder that because of the many conversations he had had with the assassin, he could reassure him and 'the Sovereign' that there could be no doubt about the truth of his statements. Furthermore, Butterworth went further with Bellingham. He wrote down a declaration in his notebook and asked Bellingham to sign it. He had no hesitation in agreeing to do so:

'John Bellingham most solemnly as in the presence of Almighty God declares that no person whatever had any knowledge of his intention to injure Mr Perceval – that he had no personal enmity against him & that it was for no sort of political motive or feeling whatever, but merely on his own private affairs that he was induced to commit the act.

Signed: John Bellingham'

Not only did Bellingham sign it but in the presence of Newman, the head keeper and one of his staff, he read it aloud 'in a firm voice' before doing so. He also contradicted a report that was apparently circulating that 'two men gave him an intimation of Mr Perceval's approach'. He then discussed the £20 promissory note. He made a clear statement:

'Mr Wilson of Stepney had called upon him that morning [the day of the assassination] for £20 on a Russian claim and for no other purpose.'

He confirms the detail of purchasing the pistols from Beckwith 'after he had given notice at Bow Street'. He then adds another interesting detail. Bellingham explained why he had not run away after the shooting; he believed that would be 'an act of assassin!' (Butterworth's own exclamation mark) Butterworth considered, with great insight, this showed 'his deluded mind been worked up this desperate deed'. He ended the letter with another assurance that there was no conspiracy. In the Home Office records, there is a note sent to Beckett who had already dealt with Bellingham, that a man called 'Wilson' had run from the House of Commons when Bellingham fired the shot and that he was known to the Bow Street man Vickery. Vickery was asked about the matter and he informed Beckett that Mrs Robarts said that Wilson had indeed called on Bellingham on the day of the murder 'about a debt'. However, he was never at the House of Commons. Mr Statham, of the Town Clerk's office at Liverpool, in a letter dated 20 May 1812 to Ryder at the Home Office, also confirms the visit, informing him that Mrs Bellingham did not know who he was. In the same letter, he also states that there is no money to be found in his Liverpool house and if there is any in London belonging to Bellingham, Mrs Bellingham would like it. It is almost certain that we can accept this declaration by Bellingham as he faced his death as true. We can also see from what happened to his family that there were no great sums of money left by him. Whilst a great number of people may well have been glad to see Perceval dead, it is unlikely they had any conspiratorial connection to Bellingham. One commentator in 1812 summed up the assassination and its cause:

'On this ground, it has been observed, that every crime has its shade; and that even assassination, the greatest of all crimes, so universally condemned, has its distinctions, which lessen, in the general estimation of mankind, the enormity of its guilt! Further with respect to Mr. Bellingham, whose part has been so fatally conspicuous in the life of Mr. Perceval, it has been observed, that, if he had been one of those political assassins recommended by some of the venal prints; or, if, on the other hand, he had been engaged by France or America to exterminate the man, whom they- consider (no matter how erroneously) as the great obstacle to peace, there would then have been no difference of opinion respecting the atrocity of a doctrine so diabolical by its practical effects on the first minister of the country. And yet the unfortunate man who could deliberately devote himself to certain death, and his children to the chance of infamy and want, rather than suffer the love of life to soften his resentment, though an acute sufferer, was perhaps not many degrees more so than hundreds of his survivors, who, like him, have experienced the sad reverses of a declining commerce.'

Chapter 16

The Question of Sanity

The question of Bellingham's insanity was raised at the time of the trial. His condition of possible emotional detachment and persecutory delusion was noted above. Now we turn to consider if he was insane. This is not the place for an academic treatment of insanity and the criminal law but in seeking to create a portrait of the assassin, his state of mind is important. The matter of insanity of a person has been around as long as man has walked on the earth; Egyptian, Babylonian and Biblical references can be found. There have always been stories and records of people who did not meet the standards of 'normality', however it was defined by any given society. R.D. Laing continually argued against prevailing trends in diagnosing mental illness and disputed how conclusions as to mental illness were reached. The arguments of the condition were no different in 1812 and even today, in our more enlightened age, there is generally better care and support. There are also the ideas of 'medical insanity' and 'legal insanity' to consider. They are not both the same. A psychiatrist may determine a person is suffering from a physical condition that may render him insane, but a jury would still have to accept that the person carried out an act whilst he was rationally unable to determine his actions as right or wrong.

It was Socrates in 404BC who noted there should be a place for those deemed 'mad', 'the offspring of the inferior, or of the better when the chance to be deformed, will be put away in some mysterious place, as they should be'. In England, as far as we can tell from the records, those considered insane often did not even reach any trial in court but were placed in the care of an institution or religious order. Socrates would have approved. If they did reach trial it was a matter of chance whether they would be committed as 'lunatic' or at times found guilty and punished. It was around 1339 that some sense of law was brought to the matter. In Edward II's reign the matter of property of a person considered insane was an issue that required legal definition. Sir William Blackstone wrote:

'A lunatic, or *non compos mentis*, is one who has had understanding, but by disease, grief, or other accident has lost the use of his reason. A lunatic is indeed properly one that has lucid intervals; sometimes enjoying his senses, and sometimes not, and that frequently depending upon the change of the moon. But under the general name of *non compos mentis* (which Sir Edward Coke says is the most legal name) are comprised not only lunatics, but persons under frenzies; or who lose their intellects by disease; those that grow deaf, dumb, and blind, not being born so; or such, in short, as are by any means rendered incapable of conducting their own affairs. To these also, as well as idiots, the king is guardian, but to a very different purpose. For the law always imagines that these accidental misfortunes may be removed; and therefore only constitutes the crown a trustee for the unfortunate persons, to protect their property, and to account to them for all profits received, if they recover, or after their decease to their representatives'.

This background directs us to consider Bellingham's case. Documents in the government's files on Bellingham point to other cases in law. One was the murder of Lord Onslow by Edward Arnold. Arnold had walked up to Onslow, who was returning from a fox hunt, and shot him at close range, similar to the action of Bellingham with Perceval. Also like Bellingham, there was no doubt he did it, there being several witnesses and Arnold's acceptance of the deed. Onslow was not dead and Arnold tried to attack him again and was restrained. Arnold had made enquires earlier that day as to his victim's whereabouts and tried to purchase a larger shot for his musket. At the trial, Arnold pleaded 'not guilty'. The question arose as to his mental status at the time of the attack. He believed that Onslow had sent imps to plague him and constantly disturb him. Witnesses appeared for both sides. The brothers and sisters of Arnold stated that he was a madman who was ill-natured and nonsensical for years. Witnesses who had seen him earlier in the day, spoke of him as 'never seeming mad' to them. No experts were called.

Judge Robert Tracy's guidance to the jury is important when we look at Bellingham and his trial judge's direction. The prosecution had a copy of this statement and they had heavily underlined passages:

'The shooting of Lord Onslow, which is the fact for which this prisoner is indicted, is proved beyond all manner of contradiction; but whether this shooting was malicious, that depends up on the sanity of the man. That he shot, and that wilfully [is proved]: but whether maliciously, that is the thing: that is the question; whether this man hath the use of his reason and sense? If he was under the visitation of God and could not distinguish between good and evil, and did not know what he did though he committed the greatest offense, yet he could not be guilty of any offense against any law whatsoever … If a man be deprived of his reason, and consequently of his intention, he cannot be guilty; and if that be the case, though he had actually killed my Lord Onslow, he is exempted from punishment; punishment is intended for example, and to deter other persons from wicked designs; but the punishment of a madman, a person that hath no design, can have no example. This is on one side. On the other side, we must be very cautious... When a man is guilty of a great offence, it must be very plain and clear, before a man is allowed such an exemption; therefore it is not every kind of frantic humour or something unaccountable in a man's actions, that points him out to be such a madman as it is to be exempted from punishment: it must be a man that is totally deprived of his understanding and memory, and doth not know what is doing, no more than an infant, than a brute, or a wild beast, such a one is never the object of punishment. Therefore I must leave it to your consideration whether the condition this man was in, as it was represented to you on one side or t'other does shew a man who knew what he was doing and was able to distinguish whether he was doing good or evil, understood what he did. And it is to be observed he was a lunatic not an idiot that is born so never recovers but a lunatic may, and hath his intervals, and they admit he was a lunatic, you are to consider what he was at this day when he committed this fact.'

Despite appearing mad with the idea of 'imps being sent by Onslow', Arnold was found guilty and sentenced to death and only reprieved on the intervention of Lord Onslow himself. The prosecution at Bellingham's trial were going to use this 'wild beast' test, as it became known, to show that Bellingham was fully sane. They also stressed that he was sane on 'the day of the fact'. However, another case in 1800 had challenged the 'wild beast' test. This was the case of James Hadfield, an ex-soldier who had been attacked by the enemy and had received severe sword wounds to his head. The wounds were such that it was reported his 'brain membrane could be seen'. He became mentally ill, from both physical and psychological trauma. He suffered delusions and believed he had contact with God and that the end of the world was soon. He came to the belief that he had to sacrifice himself to save the world. For religious reasons, he could not commit suicide and decided to publicly assassinate George III and to suffer death as a result. In other aspects of his life Hadfield could be seen to act rationally. He declared that he never wanted to harm the king but that it was his own personal way to achieve his aims. His attempt failed and he was arrested and brought to trial for treason.

His lawyer, Thomas Erskine, knew that the 'wild beast test' would not stand so he introduced the idea of 'irresistible impulse'. In summary, he argued that the delusions of his client gave him an irresistible impulse to attack the king. He called a great number of expert witnesses to support his claims. The judge intervened half way through the defence's case and it was agreed by him, the defence and the prosecution that a plea of 'not guilty' would be accepted. The jury considered this on the instructions of the judge and Hadfield was found not guilty. He was then released from legal custody into the Bethlehem Mental Hospital, where Bellingham's own father had been a resident. It was this case that led to the first act on lunacy, 'An act for the safe custody of insane persons charged with offences'. One comment from Erskine in this case was a matter for Bellingham's defence team:

> 'I admit that nothing like insanity appeared to those who examined him
> … but insane persons frequently appear in the utmost state of ability and
> composure, even in the highest paroxysms of insanity'

What is clear about Bellingham is that he was indeed capable and did 'frequently appear in the utmost state of ability'. He sincerely believed in his campaign for 'justice' and was convinced that he should have received compensation in Russia for his troubles. There was a certainty of belief that the British ambassador and his staff did not support him. Therefore, the conclusion he reached was that the British government was responsible to make good that compensation. He had tried every avenue in Russia and back in England tried to bring his case to the notice of the decision makers in parliament. Spencer Perceval had been the final gateway to let that happen and he refused Bellingham his petition. Furthermore, in his attempt to change minds he was finally told to do whatever he felt was right. In his mind, the logical way to get to court was by killing Perceval and there he sincerely believed he would be acquitted by the jury, who would understand his sufferings. Behind all this, we have also seen a religious thread that had convinced Bellingham that what he was doing would not only be judged by people to be just, but that God Himself would also agree. It is true to say that he was obsessive in his belief.

In this state was Bellingham suffering from an obsessive delusion? The definition of *non compos mentis* in legal terms has various interpretations, one of which is 'not having control of one's mind'. If Bellingham was suffering from delusion was he therefore not having control of his mind? Whilst he certainly could not meet the 'wild beast test' did he meet the 'irresistible impulse' test of Erskine? These questions were never raised in the trial because no expert witnesses were called. From a psychological perspective, there is a need to start with the fact that behaviour, whether *autonomic or deliberate* is a result of the internal mental processes of the individual. The central feature of delusion is the extent to which the person is convinced in his own mind that the belief is true. A person with a delusion will stay steadfast to the belief despite evidence to the contrary. In this state, the individual does not recognise that the obsessions or compulsions are excessive or unreasonable. Individuals holding such delusions can often appear in everyday life to act normally. It is only in their actions related to the delusion, their true mental state is revealed. This may well be the case with Bellingham. Take the example already referred to when he met Mr Smith in the presence of Mrs Billet and his wife:

"'Sir, my friends say that I am out of my senses, is it your opinion, Mr. Smith, that I am so?"

'Mr. Smith said, "It is a very delicate question for me to answer, I only know you upon this business, and I can assure you, that you will never have what you are pursuing after."'

There is no doubt what Smith said. It was plain. However, the fact that Bellingham immediately told his wife that he has just been told he will have what he was pursuing may suggest that his delusion has taken control and impaired his mental state and thus his strange response. The alternative was that he was simply being cold and deceitful and intent to keep up a determined plan to get a fortune. But why then in his trial did he shy away from a claim of insanity which may have assisted in his acquittal?

From a 'normal' perspective, he mostly acted and behaved like any other member of society, except when Russia is mentioned as we have seen above. The many reports from other observers confirm it is in relation to Russia that he displayed irrational behaviour and emotions. The killing of Perceval was the ultimate action in his delusion. Again, no expert witnesses were called to test this theory. Kathleen S Goddard in an excellent paper on the matter wrote:

'The difficulty in Bellingham's ease is that little evidence was adduced at his trial in relation to his mental state, particularly as the application for a delay to enable additional evidence to be brought from Liverpool and elsewhere had been refused. As a result, it is almost impossible to say with any accuracy whether he knew the difference between right and wrong, and whether murder was a crime. Since Bellingham's counsel had only been appointed on the day preceding the trial they had little time to prepare the defence, and assemble the necessary evidence in relation to his mental condition. Consequently, no medical evidence was produced by his counsel in relation to Bellingham's state of mind. Although his counsel had sought medical opinions from two doctors who had attended George III one could not appear at the trial and the other did not reply to the request for an opinion. The only evidence given in relation to Bellingham's mental condition came from Ann Billet, Mary Clarke, and the housemaid'.

Bellingham himself had stated he was not insane, but was he the best person to determine that? Henry Brougham, who was examining a witness at the time of the assassination, and who would become Lord Chancellor said of the trial, 'the trial was the greatest disgrace to English Justice'. Later he added:

'So great an outrage on justice never was witnessed in modern times: for the application to delay the trial until evidence of his insanity could he brought from Liverpool, was refused, and the trial proceeded, while both the court, the witnesses, the jury, and the people, were under the influence of the feelings naturally excited by the deplorable slaughter of one of the most eminent and virtuous men in any rank of the community.'

It is true to say that the court case was rushed, with the defence being appointed only 48 hours before the trial. Bellingham was certainly deprived of an adequate defence by twenty-first century standards. However, we must accept that the trial can only be judged by the standards of 1812. With that in mind, if Brougham, who was a distinguished lawyer at the time, had such a severe opinion of Bellingham's trial, then the process of justice for Bellingham must be called into question. This is in no way to try and excuse Bellingham or declare him innocent, it is a matter of justice being done and being seen to be done.

The only conclusion that can be reached is that what Bellingham did was an act of madness from any normal viewpoint. There is no escaping the reality that he did kill Spencer Perceval. However, what we cannot be certain of is his mental state at the time of the assassination. Unfortunately, the trial procedure did not have any expert testimony. Any speculation in the twenty-first century can only be anachronistic and inconclusive and will never resolve the question of Bellingham's sanity.

Chapter 17

The Aftermath

As much as Bellingham was the object of fascination at the trial, in death it was no different. The *Ipswich Journal* of 23 May 1812 reported:

> 'The body hung till nine o'clock, and as soon as it was cut down, was placed in a cart and covered with a sack. The assistant of the executioner, and a boy, got into the cart, and, preceded by the City Marshal, the body was conveyed up the Old Bailey, and along Newgate-street. The populace followed the cart close, and as the windows were thronged with spectators, the executioner 2 or 3 times removed the sack from the body that it might be seen. The cart turned down St. Martin's-le-Grand, up Little Britain, and the body was deposited at the house of the Beadle of the Surgeon's College, in Duke-street, West Smithfield. The populace then dispersed.'

The paper went on with a report that can only be described as over-exaggerated:

> 'So anxious were many persons to possess some of the relics of Bellingham, that the Executioner has sold the great coat in which the unhappy man was hung for 10£. The other parts of his dress have, we understand, been bought at a price equally exorbitant. Amongst other extraordinary exhibitions announced for the gratification of public curiosity at Greenwich Fair on Monday, was the pistol with which Mr. Perceval was shot! The price of admission was 6d and we understand the exhibitor, who solemnly protested he had purchased it at an immense sum, reaped no inconsiderable harvest from the credulity of John Bull and his family. It is a singular fact that after the body of Bellingham was opened, it was noticed that his heart continued to perform its functions, or in other words, to be alive for 4 hours after he was laid open. The expanding and contracting powers continued perceptible till one o'clock in the day – a proof of the steady, undismayed character which he preserved to the last gasp. It is said of some men, that the heart dies within them, but here the energies remained when life was extinct.'

It was true that many of Bellingham's possessions and clothing were sold. Indeed, there was a huge argument among government and court officials as to who should keep the pistols he had used. As to the heart still beating after four hours, this can be consigned to the realm of fantasy. *Bell's Weekly* was appalled at the rejoicing and support of Bellingham:

> 'The truth seems therefore to be, that it was the act of a most wicked and malignant nature working itself up to its highest possible pitch, and in the language of the criminal himself, maturing and familiarising a most horrible purpose to the mind, by frequent and intense meditation, and gradually formed resolution. The ultimate result, therefore, might possibly have the character of madness, in the same manner as the act of a drunken man might be immediately imputed to intoxication, but as the madness and the intoxication were the works of a preceding will, they are therefore fully imputable, and objects of human punishment.
>
> 'We have deemed it necessary to say as much, because we learn with regret, somewhat bordering on horror, that a part of the country are so forgetful of the national character and of the ordinary feelings of men, as to express exultation on this most disgraceful occurrence, and to have published and clamorously avowed their hopes of the escape of his murderer. Happily, however, this feeling is confined to the lowest and most basest part of the populace, and we feel persuaded no honest mind will acknowledge or countenance it.'

However, this view of Bellingham's wickedness was not shared by all. A correspondent to the *Examiner* wrote:

> 'The remarks of your Correspondent H. H. in your last number, under the head of Bellingham a madman, appears to me to be peculiarly well-toned and rational There is something in the bare idea of assassination so repugnant to In the feelings of humanity, that our abhorrence of the crime almost disqualifies us for the office of judging with fairness and impartiality the case of the perpetrator. Among the number of those, however, your correspondent H.H. must not lie classed, and in corroboration of the view he has taken of the subject, 1 enclose you the following extract of a letter recently received from a female friend at Liverpool. – 'I presume you have shared in the general horror excited by poor Perceval's assassination – Bellingham's long residence in this town has rendered his character a subject of interesting investigation. He has been grossly misrepresented in the public prints, for his widow and friends all bear testimony that his general character was that of strict integrity – a kind husband and father loyal in his political opinions – and punctual in the observance of religious duties. That he was insane on one subject, his Russian affairs, no one who knew him doubted. I have read the whole series of his correspondence with his wife and partner, during his late visit in London, and also the letter addressed to his wife on the eve of his execution – this last has not been

accurately given in the newspapers. The tenor of his letters proves him to have been a well-intentioned man; he speaks rationally on every subject but one, and that was always a subject of contention between his wife and him. It is but just that this unfortunate man's character should be recorded on the page of history free from every crime, save the one suffered, and that was the error of derangement. His letters were sent me by a particular friend of his afflicted widow. – I wish you could see them.'

This defence of Bellingham is almost certainly from Miss Stevens, who had access to all the letters, and it is a very generous rewriting of the actual truth of his behaviour. However, it does confirm that Russia was an important trigger in producing a deluded madness in Bellingham. Lord Granville Leveson was the object of a great deal of letters casting abuse at him and threatening his life. However, among these letters one anonymous writer, who obviously knew the Bellingham family, give a very different opinion of the assassin. Describing the murder as 'atrocious' and that Bellingham had received a 'just' punishment, he regrets that the punishment was not confined to him alone, but his 'innocent wife and children' suffered as well. He continues to note that Bellingham had left them no money and had 'squandered' it on his 'expensive stay in London'. The only thing that had been left to them 'was a name which will, as long as they exist, perpetuate his infamy and their disgrace'. He continues by reminding him that Bellingham may have well killed Gower if the opportunity arose – was that the reason for a second pistol? In thanksgiving for this deliverance, he suggests that Leveson might consider sending some support to the grieving widow and her children. The letter was sent to Liverpool to try and trace the writer. The newspapers carried reports that Bellingham was indeed a bad husband. The *Hampshire Chronicle* reported:

> 'A morning paper says that "Bellingham never had any capital of his own. His conduct to his wife had been for many years neglectful and unaffectionate. They have lived separate for a considerable length of time, and Bellingham seldom visited her but for the purpose of obtaining money, which he spent in London in urging his claims on Government. His wife is a milliner in Liverpool, with three children" His representations of neglect of Lord L Gower are totally unfounded. That Nobleman received so satisfactory a statement from the Russian Authorities of the legality of his detention, that he was precluded from interfering.'

The article has some truth in it, in that Bellingham never did seem to have any capital. It came to him from legacies and that was wasted on his many failed adventures. He was also apart from his wife for almost seven years of a fourteen year marriage. It is unlikely that he was deliberately neglectful or unaffectionate but as discussed, his detachment may have exacerbated the situation. However, that he spent so much money pursuing a lost cause whilst his wife struggled does raise questions as to his priorities. The truth was that Gower, (and Shairp) despite his reputation for self-interest, did write and try to resolve the matter and was told Bellingham had been legally detained.

Another letter to Leveson, this time signed, was from Mary Bellingham's kindly uncle James Neville. In it he thanks him for his donation of £50 (£3,250) to Mary – he had sent this in response to the anonymous letter. His opinion of her husband is made clear describing her as 'the widow of that wretched man Jo. Bellingham'. He explains that Mary and the children had gone to her father but he could not afford to keep them so they came to him at Wigan. He informed Leveson that Bellingham had sworn that he had given up his deluded claims but had lied. He regretted the time he had encouraged her to stick with Bellingham and goes on to make a powerful statement:

> '... yet in his manners he was kind to his family but in this conduct uniformly cruel – had he put the pistol to his own unworthy head, there would have been little cause for lamentation..'

Whilst James Neville thanked Leveson for his generosity, many others thought he should not have wasted money on the assassin's widow. John Neville, Mary's father, perhaps to make for a lack in his own provision, decided to arrange a Comic Opera to support Mary and the children. She was unaware of this and reacted angrily. The Dublin papers also reacted against the event and the London government were concerned that it could stir up trouble. Mary acted swiftly to disassociate herself from her father and publicly called on it not to take place and she also stated she would not profit from any money raised. She acknowledged her needs but poignantly added, 'There are other causes of distress, which can only be alleviated by time and removed by death'. As ever, Mary proved herself a woman of dignity. Mary wrote to Leveson, apologising for not writing sooner to thank him for his donation. She told him the deed of her husband had left her in a 'deplorable place'. Her concern was for 'her lovely children, all boys'. She continued:

> '... whose future Welfare and good conduct through life must depend in a great measure upon the education I shall be enabled to give them. To a generous public, I am compelled to look for assistance, now that I am deprived of every other resource, and trust that they will have the liberality to distinguish between the innocent and the guilty. My most ardent wish is to retire into the Country, there to devote my time and attention to my beloved Children. Compelled by dire necessity I was obliged on my return from Russia, where I left my unfortunate Husband in prison, to exert

myself in a line very uncongenial to my feelings, or the line of life I had been accustomed to move in. Even this has proved unsuccessful, and I am now deeply involved in the concern. I hope your Lordship will not deem me impertinent or presuming on your kindness in thus stating my unhappy situation, my character upon inquiry I trust would be found a deserving one, and if thro' your Lordship's interest the great and wealthy could be induced to contribute to alleviate sufferings almost too great for human nature, I doubt not but the feelings of their own hearts would be superior to any thanks I could offer.'

On 15 June 1813, aged 29, she married James Raymond Barker, aged 42, from Lurgan, her home town in Ireland, at Thornton-In-Craven, York and settled into a new life with him and her boys. Mary Bellingham would no longer bear the name of her now notorious husband. The Bishop's transcript of her marriage shows her name as Neville. As to her boys, they wanted to distance themselves from their father's name. James Bellingham, born in Russia in 1801, also changed his name to Neville. He never married and lived at Edmonton, Middlesex. He died there in 1872, leaving £7,000 (£726,000). The will was administered by his brother Henry. All census material that is available shows him with no occupation. The second boy, William, is a complete unknown and does not appear in any records. There was a William Neville, a doctor, from Wigan, who may be the missing child, but there is no collaborative evidence to support it was indeed Bellingham's son. Henry, who was born 11 May 1811, was baptised Henry Stevens Bellingham, on Dec 17 1812, in George's Street Congregational Church; he also subsequently changed his last name to Neville. He married Anne Bewley in Dublin and then returned to England to continue a career in his father's footstep as a Colonial Broker. He died in January 1875 and left £12,000 (£1.25m) in his will, far more than his father had ever managed. His wife Anne was the daughter of Mary Neville, the daughter of James Neville, Mary Bellingham's uncle.

Bellingham's son in the 1851 census has rejected his father's name but has followed in his profession.

John Bellingham comes out of history as a tragic character. He believed that he would obtain property and wealth from his crusade but instead lost everything, even his very life. To search for some good that came out of this episode in history is vain. There are two families who lost fathers and suffered that deep loss. There is a broken man and a broken family who at that time were held in opprobrium. There can be no way to justify anyone with a personal grievance taking their own justice, otherwise society moves to chaos and anarchy. The only glimmer that can be found is in the attitude to mental disturbance that the case threw up. The future would bring a more just means of assessing those accused of crimes and their mental state. The final question left is that whilst Bellingham got what many thought was due to him, does he deserve our condemnation or our pity?

If there is any certainty in the life of this man, it is that he lost himself in the miserable depths of a Russian prison. On leaving his confinement he entered a world of fantasy of his own making. He lost the compass of rationality and was guided by a star of delusion. In a desert of hopelessness, he stumbled from mirage to mirage until he found there was no water to satisfy him. He could not see the deception of the delusion and eventually he reached a sea of reality in the courts of England. Throwing himself into its depths, in the waves of the storm, he was overwhelmed. The imagined rescue of his delusion never came and death confirmed his tragic state. All that was left were broken hearts and the shattered dreams of a family and for him the name – JOHN BELLINGHAM, ASSASSIN.

Bibliography & Sources

BAILEY, J, *Trial of John Bellingham for the murder of the Right Hon. S. Perceval*, J Bailey, London, 1812.

BLACKSTONE, Sir William, *Commentaries on the Laws of England*, *(Book 1, Chapter 8, "Of the Rights of Persons")*, J P Lippincott & Co, Philadelphia, 1893.

BROUGHAM Lord Henry, *Historical sketches of statesmen who flourished in the time of George III*, Philadelphia, 1839.

BROUGHAM Lord Henry, *The Life and Times of Henry Lord Brougham*, Harper Brothers, New York, 1871.

CASSELL, PETTER & GALPIN, *Cassell's Illustrated History of England*, London, 1874.

CLARKE, W, *Trial of John Bellingham for the murder of the Right Hon. S. Perceval*, J Norton, London, 1812.

COOKE, George Wingrove, *The History of The Party*, John Macrone, London, 1837.

FIOTT, John, *Address to the Proprietors of East India Stock*, J Johnson, 1740.

FRASER, Mr, & **MERCER**, R., *Trial of John Bellingham for the assassination of the Right Hon. Spencer Perceval*, McMillan, London, 1812.

GILLEN, Molly, *Assassination of the Prime Minister*, Sidgwick & Jackson Ltd, London, 1972.

HANLEY, *An Authentic Account of the Horrid Assassination of the Right Hon. Spencer Perceval*, Allbut & Gibbs, London, 1812.

HATCHARD J, *Cursory Remarks*, J Hatchard, London, 1812.

HODGSON Thomas, *A Full and Authentic Report of the Trial of John Bellingham*, Sherwood, Neely & Jones, London, 1812.

KNAPP, Andrew & **BALDWIN** William, *The Newgate Calendar*, J Robins & Co, London, 1828.

LAING, R.D, *The Divided Self: An Existential Study in Sanity and Madness*, Penguin, Harmondsworth, 1960.

LINKLATER, Andro, *Why Spencer Perceval Had To Die*, Bloomsbury, London, 2012.

MULLAN, B, *Mad to be Normal: Conversations with R.D. Laing*. Free Association Books, London, 1995.

MUNROE, Alistair, *Delusional Disorder: Paranoia and Related Illnesses* Cambridge University Press; New Ed edition, 2008.

SCORESBY W Jun, *An Account of the Artic Regions*, Robinson & Co, London, 1820.

WILLIAMS, Charles Verulam, *The Life and Administration of the Right Honourable Spencer Perceval*, John Conrad, Philadelphia, 1813.

WILSON, Daniel Rev, *The Substance of a Conversation with John Bellingham*, John Hatchard, London, 1812.

Academic Papers:

GODDARD, Kathleen S, *A Case of Injustice? The Trial of John Bellingham*, in *The American Journal of Legal History*, Vol. 46, No. 1, (Jan., 2004), pp. 1-25, Oxford University Press, Oxford, 2004.

Newspapers:

Bell's Weekly Messenger
Corbett's Weekly
Courier
Derby Mercury
European Magazine
Gentleman's Magazine
Hampshire Chronicle
Hereford Journal
Hull Advertiser & Exchange Gazette
Hull Packet
Ipswich Journal
Kentish Weekly Post
Leeds Mercury
Liverpool Mercury
Lloyds List, London, 1804
London Courier and Evening Gazette
London Gazette
Morning Chronicle
Rhyl Journal
The Globe
The Times
York Herald

National Archives & British Library:

HO-40-25_2
HO-40-25_3
HO-40-29_1
HO-40-29_2
HO-42-119_1
HO-42-119_2
HO-42-119_3
HO-42-121_1
HO-42-121_2
HO-42-122_1
HO-42-122_2
HO-42-122_3
HO-42-123_1
HO-42-123_2
HO-42-123_3
HO-42-124_1
HO-42-124_2
HO-42-124_3
HO-42-131_1
HO-42-131_2
HO-42-62_1
HO-42-62_2
IS16W190245P
PRO 30_29_6_11
TS 11_224

Index